T0271431

Employee Learning in Small Organizations

Employee Learning in Small Organizations provides a clear, concise and comprehensive analysis of the theory and practice of employee learning in micro- and small enterprises. The book offers easy-to-digest theory alongside practical application advice on how to effectively engage with employee learning in small businesses. Rather than see small firms as scaled-down examples of large organizations, the book highlights the different constraints and challenges that smaller business face.

Topics include the wider framework of the political economy of skills, the impact of human resource development on small firms, employee learning, and the relationship with other human resource activities. This is a short accessible guide suitable for anyone interested in employee learning and small business human resources.

Dr Antonios Panagiotakopoulos is an associate professor of human resource management and course director for the BA in Business and HRM and MSc in HRM at Norwich Business School, University of East Anglia.

Employee Learning in Small Organizations

A Concise Guide for Small Organizations

Antonios Panagiotakopoulos

Routledge
Taylor & Francis Group

LONDON AND NEW YORK

First published 2024
by Routledge
4 Park Square, Milton Park, Abingdon, Oxon OX14 4RN

and by Routledge
605 Third Avenue, New York, NY 10158

Routledge is an imprint of the Taylor & Francis Group, an informa business

British Library Cataloguing-in-Publication Data
A catalogue record for this book is available from the British Library

ISBN: 978-1-032-46462-6 (hbk)
ISBN: 978-1-032-46465-7 (pbk)
ISBN: 978-1-003-38181-5 (ebk)

DOI: 10.4324/9781003381815

Typeset in Times New Roman
by SPi Technologies India Pvt Ltd (Straive)

Contents

About the author

Dr **Antonios Panagiotakopoulos** is an associate professor of human resource management (HRM) and course director for the BA in Business and HRM and MSc in HRM at Norwich Business School, University of East Anglia. Antonios holds a PhD in HRM from the University of Leeds, where he serves as a regular teaching and research fellow at the Centre for Employment Relations, Innovation and Change. Antonios has extensive academic, research and consulting experience both in Greece and the U.K., especially in the area of workforce skills development in the small business context. In particular, he has worked as an academic for the last 17 years teaching various modules such as Managing People, International HRM, Training and Development, Employee Relations, Organizational Behaviour and Research Methods to undergraduate and postgraduate students at the University of Leeds, the University of Chester, the New York College (Greece), the American College of Greece and the University of East Anglia. During his career, he has won several teaching and research awards, whilst his articles have been published in various international peer-reviewed academic journals including the *International Journal of Training and Development*, the *Journal of Business Strategy*, *The Learning Organization*, the *Journal of Workplace Learning* and others.

Acknowledgements

This book is dedicated to Maria. Her endless love, continuous encouragement and support have been vital for the completion of this effort. I further extend my gratitude to my beloved parents, my sister and her family and a few close friends for their enthusiastic support. My mentors Prof. Mark Stuart and Prof. Christopher Forde (both at Leeds University), as well as Dr Susan Sayce (University of East Anglia [UEA]) deserve my special thanks for their valuable guidance during my academic career. Also, I wish to thank deeply Dr Josie Kinge (an excellent colleague at UEA) for all the precious knowledge-sharing activities in our modules, as well as Alexander McGregor (my editor at Routledge) for believing in this effort from the very first moment. Last but not least, I would like to thank my grandmother Stamatia Kostopoulou, who was the first mentor of my life.

Aims of the book and significance

As the title suggests, this book provides a concise analysis of the skills development process of employees in small organizations. It is a short textbook designed for busy small firm owners/managers that wish to facilitate staff learning in the workplace. Essentially, it seeks to outline the purpose and operation of human resource development (HRD) activities in the small business context by adopting a critical perspective. It aims to provide practitioners with an understanding not only of the potential for HRD to contribute to improved organizational performance and individual well-being at work but also why it very often fails to such positive outcomes. The ultimate aim of this book is to raise the awareness of small firm owners on how to develop human talent that will drive organizational success.

Furthermore, both undergraduate and postgraduate students of a subject like Employee Development, which draws on several of the social sciences, are likely to be helped by a concise textbook that focuses on small establishments. The idea throughout the book is to facilitate students' efforts to match their reading to their future job-related tasks in the wider area of employee learning. At the end of each chapter, there is a reflective case study that may help both practitioners and students understand how theory can be put into practice.

Organization of Study

The present textbook is structured as follows: In the introductory chapter, the main goals and central focus of this publication are outlined and its significance is discussed. In Chapter 1, a critical review of the relevant literature is undertaken, investigating the political economy of skills to help readers understand the general context of workforce skills development. In Chapter 2, the wider social and financial impact of staff learning is extensively discussed. Several empirical studies are presented to outline the importance of skills development for individuals, organizations and society. Also, an analysis is conducted on how employee learning can help small firm owners manage change effectively in today's turbulent business world. The process of informal learning in small establishments is discussed thoroughly in Chapter 3, whereas in Chapter 4, the interlinking of some other core human resource management activities (e.g. staff selection, performance appraisal, rewards) with employee learning is examined. In Chapter 5, the concept of leadership is explored and its importance for the effective acquisition of job-related skills is examined. Finally, in Chapter 6, the analysis moves on to explore the impact of cross-cultural differences across the world on employee informal learning. The concluding chapter summarizes the core arguments of the present publication in relation to employee learning and development.

Introduction

Across the world, the need for better-trained employees is even more acute at a time when most governments are attempting to improve the living standards of their citizens and provide employment opportunities for all. The quality of human capital plays a key role in productivity growth, but several countries in the global arena suffer from a lack of high-skilled workers and poor people management practices. Nowhere is this more acute than in the small business sector, particularly for those micro-firms (i.e. firms with less than 10 employees) in several sectors of economic activity, which experience fierce national and international competition (Panagiotakopoulos, 2020a). In several parts of the advanced world, the main problems facing such firms are widely acknowledged in political and academic circles and include low product quality, high production costs, low capital investment, organizational inadequacies, a lack of high-skilled personnel and weak supportive structures. Such problems in conjunction with competitive pressures from low-cost producers in developing countries and several other external factors (e.g. pandemic, environmental concerns, technological changes) have led to the closure of thousands of small firms across the world and high levels of labour displacement (Mazzarol and Reboud, 2020).

In order to survive, it is frequently argued by policy makers that the small business sector needs to develop a more careful approach to the planning and implementation of employee learning interventions. The very intense competition from foreign markets due to globalization has forced firms to build intelligent systems of labour and machines that are flexible and can quickly respond to the desires of the market. In this context, human capital constitutes a major component of business success and employee learning becomes a necessity. In short, investment in workforce skills development becomes important in terms of responding quickly to technological and product change, as well as in terms of more social concerns such as worker retention and employability.

It has been noted in the literature that human resource development (HRD) theory often suggests solutions relating to workforce training

DOI: 10.4324/9781003381815-1

which are practical only for large establishments having personnel specialists with the time and experience to implement suggested delivery. However, a number of aspects of human resource training and development activity have the potential to be of particular interest to small enterprises both because of their restricted resources and the need to be responsive to the fast-changing demands of the marketplace. Highly motivated, developing staff with effective transferable skills are more likely to be able to meet the demands of the fast-changing environment which is typically associated with small businesses (Kerr and McDougall, 1999; Panagiotakopoulos, 2009).

Despite the importance of workforce training for all business organizations, the majority of the literature in the HRD field continues to emphasize large firms, even though their economic significance has declined in recent years. Little effort is made toward understanding how small enterprises approach training and generating models of effective practice. This gives a distorted picture of the industrial landscape, masking the fundamental importance of small firms as a source of employment and as contributors to a dynamic economy (Hendry *et al.*, 1995). A whole range of authors have bemoaned the lack of attention within the HRD literature that is given to small enterprises and have pointed out that such under-representation seems inappropriate when the scale of this sector is considered (Matlay, 1997; Kerr and McDougall, 1999; Johnson, 2002; Panagiotakopoulos, 2020b).

It should be pointed out that small firms are not '*scaled-down*' versions of large firms and they face different motivations, constraints and uncertainties from their large counterparts (Westhead and Storey, 1996, p. 18). As a result, HRD practices in such firms are different from those in large establishments, and hence, these organizations should be analysed specifically in academic research. As Matlay (1997) wisely noted in the past, attempts to down-scale and forcibly fit large-scale training strategies to resource-starved small businesses may result in drawing misleading conclusions regarding the nature, extent and determinants of staff learning in small organizations. A rigorous examination of the existing literature reveals that there is not much empirical knowledge of HRD in small firms, and as a result, there is no accurate information about the nature, extent, drivers and obstacles of learning in such establishments (Panagiotakopoulos, 2020b). In the absence of reliable data, learning improvement efforts can only take place by trial and error. Against this background, this publication comes to fill this significant lacuna.

The scant empirical evidence in the small business context has shown that workplace learning is deemed crucial for the 'upskilling' of small business employees in order to increase their ability to produce high-quality goods and services. Moreover, it contributes significantly to small firm survival and growth by enabling small enterprises to meet skill shortage needs, it raises employee confidence, it promotes a good atmosphere at work, it increases workforce flexibility, trust and loyalty and it reduces staff turnover, as well as leads to product and service innovation (Hendry *et al.*, 1995; Kitching and Blackburn, 2002; Panagiotakopoulos, 2011).

One of the most important trends over the past decades is undeniably the growth of insecurity in the world of work (i.e., precariousness). World-wide, an increasing number of workers suffer from precarious, insecure, uncertain and unpredictable working conditions that affect their overall well-being (Standing, 2014). Several terms have appeared in the literature that denote this fundamental economic and societal change, including the 'gig economy' (i.e. the increased tendency for businesses to hire independent contractors and short-term workers), zero-hours working (a term used to describe a type of employment contract between an employer and an employee whereby the employer is not obliged to provide any minimum number of working hours to the employee), remote working (a working style that allows professionals to work outside of a traditional office environment) and talent sharing (i.e., one employer 'shares' workers who would otherwise lose their jobs with another employer that desperately needs workers to meet unexpected business demand; Woodcock and Graham, 2020). In this context, continuous employee learning features as a key element in an individual's effort to enhance their job security since skills development can make workers employable. To this end, it is important to explore how small firm owners can support this process, which radically affects staff motivation.

In-work poverty has also emerged as another major social implication closely linked to precariousness at work. For a long time, in-work poverty was not associated with European states, and having a job used to be perceived as the most effective prevention mechanism against falling into poverty. In this context, the fact that people might suffer from poverty even though they were in full-time employment was left out of account in most research studies around poverty. This view changed gradually during the last decade, and the particular topic has drawn increasing attention as a potential consequence of recent studies, which have revealed that in-work poverty significantly affects individual mental well-being and happiness, as well as employee productivity. Hence, it has become a major concern for all policy makers across the globe (Spannagel, 2013; Panagiotakopoulos, 2019). The existing research studies indicate that the perception held around in-work poverty is that households are working poor because of their certain composition or the characteristics of their household members ignoring other factors such as the prevailing labour market and welfare state institutions and policies. The question of how country-level political, social or economic institutions influence in-work poverty patterns has recently started to be taken into account by research. Furthermore, the emphasis of research has been placed predominantly on the welfare state measures to fight in-work poverty, whereas the contribution of employers is underplayed. One of the very few relevant studies in this area has been undertaken by Joseph Rowntree Foundation in 2014, pointing to the fact that certain human resource management (HRM) practices, including staff training, could help employers tackle in-work poverty. Similar results were reported in a later study conducted by Richards and Sang (2015) in Scotland and Panagiotakopoulos (2019) in Greece, where the authors found that if employers could provide their staff with access to affordable credit (e.g., an emergency loan to cover immediate expenses) and training, they could help them to overcome the burden of in-work poverty.

It is therefore worth exploring how small-firm learning provisions can address in-work poverty. For example, if employer practices can be demonstrated to reduce employee stress, assist progression in work and boost income in ways other than through direct pay, it may be that they can have a positive impact on staff experiencing poverty or at risk of poverty. Furthermore, if a business case can be constructed for 'making bad jobs better', it will be possible to encourage small firm owners to tackle poverty among their workforce. Against this background, this publication explores the path through which small firm organizations can become 'anti-poverty employers' by adopting employee-friendly HRM practices, including systematic performance appraisals, extensive workplace learning and the provision of various non-financial benefits that could improve the overall quality of working life for employees.

The need for an adaptable workforce is here to stay. The new employment landscape forces all organizations to rethink traditional employee development practices and adopt new talent management practices. The way employees are selected, trained, appraised and motivated in this new business environment differs radically from the past decades. Hence, the present publication is an attempt to present new ways of managing and developing talent in this new era with a special reference to small organizations that continue to face several constraints and huge challenges in this unstable business environment. Small firms do play a vital role in the economic growth of most economies around the globe, so their study acquires a unique urgency.

Talent development is affected by a range of internal and external factors including corporate culture, chosen business strategy, selection and reward systems, labour market collective organizations, national educational systems, international competition, technological advances, environmental changes and so on. All these variables should be taken into account when discussing employee learning (Ashton and Green, 1996; Panagiotakopoulos, 2020b). Against this backdrop, this book adopts a holistic approach to HRD interventions and addresses some fundamental concerns on the importance of talent development to small firm strategies.

It further informs small firm owners on how to create tailor-made and cost-effective learning opportunities for their employees, thus remaining competitive in both the domestic and international markets.

The present effort breaks new ground in various respects. First, it helps readers understand how HRD interventions in small firms can contribute to the economic development of several countries across the world. Second, it examines all the key factors that determine the level and intensity of training in small firms. Existing studies around the forces that trigger training have concentrated on large organizations. However, this publication operates from the premise that small firms are not microcosms of large firms, and as such require separate treatment. It is inappropriate and inadequate simply to apply large-firm logic to small organizations. Hence, this study attempts to deepen our knowledge about the reasons why some small firms train and others do not, as well as understand why some small organizations do get positive organizational outcomes from workforce skills development and others do not. Finally, the study explores how the process of talent development in the small business context could be further supported and enhanced with the contribution of other HR core practices such as selection, performance appraisal, rewards and employee relations.

Key points of the chapter

The global business environment has become very unpredictable. Frequent changes at the operational and strategic levels are needed by all types of organizations in order to respond effectively to the numerous challenges posed by the external environment and achieve competitive advantage in their markets. The need is even greater for small enterprises that suffer from resource poverty and cannot cope easily with unexpected external events.

Employee learning remains one of the critical factors for small-firm success. Small organizations need to unleash their innovative capacity to survive and stay ahead of the competition. Yet, innovation cannot be achieved on the basis of low-skilled labour. Therefore, skills development acquires a unique urgency.

References

Ashton, D. and F. Green (1996) *Education, training and the global economy*. Cheltenham: Edward Elgar.

Hendry, C., Arthur, M. B. and Jones, A. M. (1995) *Strategy through people: adaptation and learning in the small-medium enterprise*. London: Routledge.

Johnson, S. (2002) 'Lifelong learning and SMEs: issues for research and policy', *Journal of Small Business and Enterprise Development*, vol. 9, no. 3, pp. 285–295.

Joseph Rowntree Foundation (2014) *Rewarding work for low-paid workers*. York: JRF Publications.

Kerr, A. and M. McDougall (1999) 'The small business of developing people', *International Small Business Journal*, vol. 17, no. 2, pp. 65–74.

Kitching, J. and R. Blackburn (2002) *The nature of training and motivation to train in small firms*. Department for Education and Skills (DfES), Research report No 330. Nottingham: DfES publications.

Matlay, H. (1997) 'The paradox of training in the small business sector of the British economy', *Journal of Vocational Education and Training*, vol. 49, no. 4, pp. 573–589.

Mazzarol, T. and S. Reboud (2020) *Small business management*. 4th ed. Singapore: Springer Publications.

Panagiotakopoulos, A (2009) 'An empirical investigation of employee training and development in Greek manufacturing SMES', PhD thesis, University of Leeds.

Panagiotakopoulos, A. (2011) 'Workplace learning and its organizational benefits for small enterprises: evidence from Greek industrial firms', *The Learning Organization*, vol. 18, no. 5, pp. 364–374.

Panagiotakopoulos, A. (2019) 'In-work poverty: reversing a trend through business commitment', *Journal of Business Strategy*, vol. 40, no. 5, pp. 3–11.

Panagiotakopoulos, A. (2020a) 'Exploring the link between management training and organizational performance in the small business context', *Journal of Workplace Learning*, vol. 32, no. 4, pp. 245–257.

Panagiotakopoulos, A. (2020b) *Effective workforce development: a concise guide for HR and line managers*. London: Routledge Publications.

Richards, J. and K. Sang (2015) 'In-work poverty: lessons for employers and HR practictioners', Paper presented at the *CIPD conference for applied research*, London, 8th December 2015.

Spannagel, D. (2013) '*In-work poverty in Europe: extent, structure and causal mechanisms*', COPE project. Luxembourg: European Commission Publications.

Standing, G. (2014) *The precariat: the new dangerous class*. London: Bloomsbury Academic.

Westhead, P. and D. Storey (1996) 'Management training and small firm performance: why is the link so weak?', *International Small Business Journal*, vol. 14, no. 4, pp. 13–24.

Woodcock, J. and M. Graham (2020) *The gig economy: a critical introduction*. Cambridge: Polity Press.

1   The political economy
of skills

Skill creation systems

The intensified international competition and the rapid technological progress, which, as it spreads through industry radically upgrades the skill requirements, have made the question of how nations organize and adapt their skill formation policies to the vagaries of twenty-first-century global capitalism an urgent research question. Since the 1990s, it has witnessed an almost universal policy consensus emerging across the advanced capitalist world stressing the pursuit of a high-skill, knowledge-based economy and learning society (Crouch *et al.*, 1999).

It has been frequently argued in the HRM literature that the challenges posed by several low-cost organizations across the world can be met only if firms in advanced countries are able to produce sophisticated, high-quality products that are hard to imitate. However, productivity gains and innovation cannot be achieved on the basis of low-skilled work. Hence, employees in the advanced world need to possess a high level of skills, which will differentiate them from the knowledge of workers in less developed countries. As several authors have previously stressed, in the global economy, capital and finance are increasingly easily transferred. It is the human resource which therefore becomes the major difference between competing economies (Muhlemeyer and Clarke, 1997; Brown, 1999). When consumer preferences and technologies are changing rapidly, adaptability is crucial for keeping labour employed and maintaining competitiveness. Therefore, employee training becomes essential to equip individuals with the skills required to make themselves more productive and adaptable. Beyond that, without a workforce that is continuously acquiring new skills, managers are not able to introduce more sophisticated and productive machines, and thus, it becomes difficult to reap most of the returns from technological advances (Booth and Snower, 1996; Stavrou-Costea, 2005).

DOI: 10.4324/9781003381815-2

It should be pointed out that although a new production system has emerged in many countries based on high quality, quick response and high value-added product strategies, which stands in contrast with the standardized low value-added production system that dominated the twentieth century, yet a significant number of firms across various economic sectors still choose to compete primarily on the basis of low-priced, standardized goods and services and a predominantly low-skill, low-wage and casualized workforce. It remains debatable whether organizations have only one viable 'high-value' route to competitiveness and profitability or whether the 'low-cost' pathway remains a viable option for many of them. As it has been argued in the past, delocalization of production to developing countries in order to reduce costs can be the preferred business strategy for many organizations operating in labour-intensive sectors in advanced capitalist economies (Keep and Mayhew, 1999).

Despite the existence of alternative forms of competition, it has been stressed by several academics that organizations in the more advanced capitalist states need to invest in innovation to face the fierce competition from low-cost producers and achieve an above-average return (Green, 1998; Mayhew and Neely, 2006). For example, increased labour costs in many labour-intensive sectors of the European industry have prevented small and large firms from competing on the basis of low-quality, low-cost goods. In contrast, new technologies promise lucrative business applications, and thus, firms are being encouraged to innovate. It has been shown that the most successful organizations in such sectors (e.g. textiles, clothing) are those companies that rely on unique brands.

In simple terms, the evidence suggests that the most successful small enterprises in most sectors have been those firms that rely on innovation and the creation of unique brands (i.e. creation of *niche* markets). In such markets, customers have a distinct set of needs, and they are willing to pay a premium price to the firm that best satisfies their needs. As a result, firms have a great potential for profit and growth (Panagiotakopoulos, 2015). Furthermore, the 'high skills route' features as a more desirable path for policy makers given the social and distributional outcomes since along the 'high-skills path' the fruits of economic success are widely distributed (i.e. most workers gain higher wages and skills in the context of a 'learning society'), whereas along the 'low-skills path' enterprises may continue to prosper but economic success is confined to elite sections of the workforce (Keep *et al.*, 2006).

Again this background, many policy makers have viewed human resource development as the answer to a range of economic and social problems ranging from competitiveness, productivity and economic growth to unemployment and social exclusion. Across the developed world and in many developing countries too, the thought is paramount that the way to economic growth is via skill formation to raise labour productivity and hence average living standards. The search for better institutions for fostering skill formation has preoccupied policy makers (Panagiotakopoulos, 2020).

However, at the same time, there has been a broad range of criticisms about the limitations of such an approach, which rests on the simplistic notion of human capital theory and an emphasis on a very narrow set of supply-side interventions. A number of studies have recognized that the market for human resource training is located in a broader social and economic system and that change in the former must be viewed in relation to its impact on the latter (Finegold and Soskice, 1988; Keep and Mayhew, 1999).

Finegold and Soskice (1988), for example, several decades ago argued that change in just one part of the socio-economic system is unlikely to be successful if the rest of the system remains the same. They showed this by reference to the 'low-skill equilibrium'. In this situation, a number of mutually reinforcing mechanisms, emanating from a variety of sources, constrain the economy to a low skill level. Change in any one of these, which is aimed at increasing the level of skill formation will not succeed because the other forces, many of which operate outside the training market, will mitigate its effect. They therefore pointed to a broad approach to policy change rather than one focused on eradicating perceived imperfections within the training market.

Several other studies attempted to explore and understand the relationship between social institutions, production strategies, skill formation and economic competitiveness, particularly in a comparative context (Ashton and Green, 1996). Starting from a rejection of human capital theory, they stressed the need for a holistic and multi-disciplinary approach to theorizing skill formation, emphasizing both the demand for and supply of skills. Attention was then focused on the institutional linkages between government agencies, the education and training system, labour market regulations, employment structures and systems of finance and industrial relations that help shape the skill trajectory of a particular country. The issue of workplace industrial relations also remained largely absent from the skills debate. Many policies did not directly deal with what happened at the workplace and could not be expected to lead automatically to a high-quality working environment. Employers, for example, appeared to select a high-quality product route but with the vast majority of employees undertaking a narrow range of tasks, with limited job autonomy and little real involvement in work (Grugulis, 2003).

The trend in the skills literature is often to assume that firms only need to move 'up-market', and they will automatically require a higher-skilled workforce. A high-quality or high-value-added product may enable the use of such a workforce, but there is no guarantee. Lloyd and Payne (2002) have pointed out that the power relations within the firm, in conjunction with wider institutional constraints, play a key role in the development of forms of work organization and skill levels. Locating issues of class, conflict and power at the centre of the skills debate is crucial for any project that realistically aims to shift the economy onto some high-skills, high-wage trajectory.

The preceding analysis underscores the necessity of a high-skill strategy and the need to maximize the role of high-productivity labour if living standards in advanced countries are to be sustained and improved. As it has been repeatedly argued by most commentators in this field, the challenges posed by the rise of low-cost producers in other parts of the world can be met only if labour in advanced countries has a high level of skills, which will differentiate it from the capacities of workers in the newly industrializing countries. Ashton and Green (1996, p. 191) have added that the high-skill route emphasizes the role of education and training as a powerful means for ensuring the full realization of human capabilities and offers '*a substantial expansion of freedoms that accrue to a well-educated and highly trained population*'. Moreover, education has a vital role to play towards creating a more sophisticated consumer base across the world with an emphasis on product/service quality. Furthermore, Finegold (1991) has stressed that it is in the interest of individuals, employers and policymakers to strive for a high-skill equilibrium since individuals can ensure higher future wages and more rewarding jobs, employers will be enabled to maintain and increase their competitive edge through improved quality, flexibility and innovation while the government policy makers can improve international competitiveness without a decline in the living standards of the average voter.

The available evidence further suggests that there is a need for a holistic approach to theorizing skill formation, emphasizing both the demand for and supply of skills. A skilled and well-educated workforce is a vital ingredient of any advanced economy, but equally important is the fact that there are enough skilled jobs for workers to do. Attention should focus on the institutional connections between government agencies, the education and training system, labour market regulations, systems of finance and industrial relations that help shape the skill trajectory of firms. This suggests that any governmental and employer policies should encompass a wider set of measures that affect all the main variables involved in the socio-economic system in order to support a 'high-skills' path.

Reflective Case Study

'*Bank U*' is a leading player in the U.K. retail banking sector with a market share of about 20%. The bank's business strategy is to aggressively grow its call centre and internet businesses while shrinking the branch network. It intends to market itself based on an image of quality (which it hopes will be backed up by the service provided to customers) with affordable costs. It has rejected the option of offshoring call centre operations because of concerns that this would compromise the image of quality that Bank U regards as a key part of its brand.

'Loan Call' is the telephone banking arm of the personal loans division of Bank U. Customers who contact the call centre wish to either apply for a personal loan (sales calls) or have a query about an existing loan (administration calls). Sales calls and administration calls come through on different telephone numbers and are dealt with by separate groups of staff. Customers are credit-scored, and loans are only made to customers who have a satisfactory credit rating. The call centre is open 7 days, from 9 a.m. to 9 p.m. There are no unsociable hours premium, and 6 workers were specially recruited to be fully flexible (getting a 20% top-up on their salary). Shifts are fully rotational. In all, 50 staff work at Loan Call centre mostly as customer service advisors (CSAs). There are also 7 team leaders and 1 call centre manager. The ratio of women/men is 70/30. All employees work full-time. The average age of staff is 25. CSAs get the national minimum wage and a 2-day induction training around their tasks.

All calls are scripted and recorded. A large LED display on the wall shows the number of calls in queue, time taken per call, sales enquiries to sales ratio and service level. CSAs are grouped into teams but because of shift work and high turnover, most do not actually sit with their teams or indeed know the other team members. The team leader, who supervises 6 CSAs, is responsible for coaching, performance management, return to work interviews, scheduling of holidays and so on, as well as working on the phones during busy periods. They are mainly responsible for ensuring that CSAs meet their targets in terms of the number of calls taken and the sales enquiries converted to sales. Loan Call has reached its target of 80% of calls to be answered in 20 seconds. However, sales targets have proved hard to meet. In terms of employee involvement, team meetings are supposed to take place twice weekly, with CSAs scheduled to be off the phones, but in practice, these often do not happen because of the volume of work. A monthly newsletter is produced to inform employees about the current situation of the company.

Problem

During the last 6 months, the staff turnover rate has dramatically increased. Exit interviews are carried out which show that morale is low and occupational stress very high. There is a lot of 1-day absence at Loan Call as well.

Tasks

1   What are the key HR issues that the senior management team should immediately address at the Loan Call centre?
2   How can employee learning be used to try to improve performance at the call centre?

Key points of the chapter

The political economy of skills has moved on significantly from the limiting assumptions of human capital theory, that improving the supply of skills will create its own demand and solve the problems of low-skill economies. Recent research has pointed to the need for a more holistic, 'societal' approach to skill formation involving the institutional linkages between government agencies, the education and training system, labour market regulation, employment structures and systems of finance and industrial relations.

A number of key societal conditions are necessary for the attainment of an ideal-type high-skills society. Among the key conditions feature a value-adding rather than a cost-cutting approach to productivity and competitiveness, the continuous development and investment in human capital and high levels of trust between employers and workers, which are embedded in the institutional fabric of society. The key argument that emerges from the discussion in this chapter is that the relationship between skill supply and demand is not a mechanistic one. This means that an increase in the skill levels of the working population does not automatically affect employer demand for a skilled workforce.

References

Ashton, D. and F. Green (1996) *Education, training and the global economy*. Cheltenham: Edward Elgar.

Booth, A. L. and D. J. Snower (1996) *Acquiring skills*. Cambridge: Cambridge University Press.

Brown, P. (1999) 'Globalisation and the political economy of high-skills', *Journal of Education and Work*, vol. 12, no. 3, pp. 233–251.

Crouch, C., Finegold, D. and Sako, M. (1999) *Are skills the answer?* Oxford: Oxford University Press.

Finegold, D. (1991) 'Institutional incentives and skill creation: preconditions for a high-skill equilibrium', in Ryan, P. (ed.) *International comparisons of vocational education and training for intermediate skills*, pp. 93–118. London: The Falmer Press.

Finegold, D. and D. Soskice (1988) 'The failure of British training: analysis and prescription', *Oxford Review of Economic Policy*, vol. 4, no. 3, pp. 21–53.

Green, F. (1998) 'Securing commitment to skill formation policies', *New Political Economy*, vol. 3, no. 1, pp. 134–139.

Grugulis, I. (2003) 'Putting skills to work: learning and employment at the start of the century', *Human Resource Management Journal*, vol. 13, no. 2, pp. 3–12.

Keep, E. and K. Mayhew (1999) 'The assessment: knowledge, skills and competitiveness', *Oxford Review of Economic Policy*, vol. 15, no. 1, pp. 1–15.

Keep, E., Mayhew, K. and Payne, J. (2006) 'From skills revolution to productivity miracle – not as easy as it sounds?', *Oxford Review of Economic Policy*, vol. 22, no. 4, pp. 539–559.

Lloyd, C. and J. Payne (2002) 'Developing a political economy of skill', *Journal of Education and Work*, vol. 15, no. 4, pp. 364–390.

Mayhew, K. and A. Neely (2006) 'Improving productivity – opening the black box', *Oxford Review of Economic Policy*, vol. 22, no. 4, pp. 445–456.

Muhlemeyer, P. and M. Clarke (1997) 'The competitive factor: training and development as a strategic management task', *Journal of Workplace Learning*, vol. 9, no. 1, pp. 4–11.

Panagiotakopoulos, A. (2015) 'Creating a high-skills society during recession: issues for policy makers', *International Journal of Training and Development*, vol. 19, no. 4, pp. 253–269.

Panagiotakopoulos, A. (2020) *Effective workforce development: a concise guide for HR and line managers*. London: Routledge Publications.

Stavrou-Costea, E. (2005) 'The challenges of human resource management towards organisational effectiveness: a comparative study in Southern EU', *Journal of European Industrial Training*, vol. 29, no. 2, pp. 112–134.

2 Employee learning and impact on small firm performance

Definition of HRD

Although several studies in the past tried to investigate the term *skill*, there is a lack of consensus about what the term means. The term *skill* frequently includes a wide range of soft, generic and transferable attributes, usually indistinguishable from personal characteristics, which in the past would never have been conceived of as skills at all. In other words, the notion of skill is now both broader and more conceptually equivocal than it has ever been. However, a basic consensus around 'skill' has emerged. Specifically, it can be argued that 'skill' includes the internalized capacities resident in the individual worker that give them control over the labour process. It is also socially constructed, which means that class, gender and race may affect how employee skills are being valued within a society (Grugulis *et al.*, 2004).

Human resource development is defined broadly as a set of activities designed by an organization to provide its members with the opportunities to learn the necessary skills to meet existing job requirements and prepare them for future job responsibilities. To put it simply, employee training comprises the procedures that seek to provide learning activities to enhance the skills, knowledge and capabilities of people, teams and the organization so that there is a change in action to achieve the desired outcomes. At the heart of training is human learning. The overall aim of workforce training is to ensure that the organization has the quality of people it needs to achieve its objectives for improved performance and growth (Panagiotakopoulos, 2020b).

After a job placement, many employees may not have the ability to perform well in their new job. Often, they must be trained in the duties they are expected to do. Even if they are experienced workers, they must be trained in order to learn about the organization and its culture, be introduced to workmates, enhance their existing skills and improve their performance. In addition, existing employees need to be trained in order to achieve and sustain superior performance. However, it should be

DOI: 10.4324/9781003381815-3

pointed out that training does more than just prepare employees to perform their jobs effectively. Training for special purposes (e.g. stress management, adjusting to staff diversity) is also required in order to help employees become aware of and cope with such issues. Moreover, the long-term development of human resources reduces the company's dependence on hiring new workers. If employees are trained and developed properly, then new job openings are likely to be filled internally. Furthermore, promotions and transfers facilitate the achievement of employee career goals and employees, in turn, feel a greater commitment to the firm and work towards the achievement of strategic business objectives (i.e. their motivation is enhanced; Noe, 2019).

Last but not least, employee training has a vital social role to play. In other words, workforce skills development enables employees to develop a range of 'transferable' skills and, thus, improve their future employment prospects (i.e. employability). Continuous employee learning can provide workers with a sense of 'job security' in today's uncertain business environment since it makes them employable. Also, as it was stressed in the introduction of this publication, it can be one of the mechanisms through which employees can be protected from in-work poverty (Panagiotakopoulos, 2019).

Workplace training and business performance

The workplace is enormously significant as a site of learning, both for accessing formal learning opportunities and for many informal learning opportunities which result from the nature of work and from social interaction with work groups. Effective training policies are fundamental to economic growth and productivity. In several major global surveys, human resource development has been found to be the most important human resources (HR) activity in all countries concerned. Although the connections between skill development and competitiveness on the one hand and productivity and prosperity on the other, are unclear, continuing training is increasingly recognized as contributing to productivity and to the management of change through the adaptation and extension of skills, on one hand, and in facilitating new patterns of work, on the other (Rainbird, 2000; Panagiotakopoulos, 2009).

A number of empirical studies have found that training has a positive effect on productivity, quality and staff turnover (DeSimone *et al.*, 2002). These studies have stressed the fact that the neglect of human resource training activity can hamper organizational performance. In attention to skills development thus is found to hamper organizational performance in a number of ways, including limiting the take-up and use of new technology, lengthening delivery times, increasing scrap levels and reducing the ability of the organization to meet increases in demand

and to exploit market opportunities. For example, investments in new technology usually demand training interventions since there are various task and skill implications of introducing new equipment. Employee training enables workers to make more effective use of the capital equipment they work with.

In the small business context specifically, all the available research studies have pointed to the importance of workforce skills development for small firms' success. In particular, the existing empirical data indicate that employee learning can help staff: reduce errors in the production process, become familiar with advanced technology (i.e. it increases their adaptability to new business processes) and improve their employability. Moreover, it leads to product and service innovation, as well as helps enterprises gain a competitive advantage in their niche markets (Kerr and McDougall, 1999; Johnson, 2002; Panagiotakopoulos, 2011).

However, as Patton *et al.* (2000) have stressed, the axiomatic proposition that training enhances business performance remains difficult to demonstrate. The range of variables in the relationship between training and organizational performance, including the external and internal context of the firms (e.g. the nature of financial markets, competitive strategy, organizational structures, labour market deregulation, management and control of the workforce, power relations between managers and workers and between different groups of workers), the nature and extent of training interventions, as well as the complexities associated with isolating the impact of training on performance, make determining extremely difficult a definite answer to the question of payback on training and the establishment of cause–effect relationships. It is still far from established that training represents the key determinant of an organization's financial performance. It is virtually impossible to establish a direct association or causal connection between training and profitability, for example.

However, it is tentatively suggested in the existing literature that, instead of positive benefits accruing to organizations which train, it is more feasible to demonstrate that organizational performance can be held back through a neglect of training activity. In particular, a lack of emphasis on workforce skills development has been found to hamper organizational performance in a number of ways, including limiting the take-up and use of new technology, lengthening delivery times, increasing error levels and reducing the ability of the organization to meet increases in demand and to exploit market opportunities (Bakhshi *et al.*, 2017).

Recent research evidence by the author also demonstrates that there is a positive relationship between owner/management training and the bottom-line performance of a small firm. In particular, the findings reveal that those small firm owners/managers who have completed a formal learning intervention do achieve positive organizational outcomes (e.g. increased staff loyalty) compared to poorly trained owners. The latter seem

2.3. Logistic audit – organization, stages, procedures

The organization and conduct of work related to the implementation of a logistics audit in an enterprise requires a sequence of activities that will make the implementation of the audit possible. On the other hand, efficiency in conducting a logistics audit will, in fact, be the result of two variables – the already-mentioned organization in its preparation, as well as knowledge about the areas that will be the subject of the auditor's research. This efficiency should be interpreted here as the possibility of a logistic audit to achieve the goal assigned to it. In the case of this type of audit, its general objective is – as already mentioned in Section 2.2 – to assess the state of the enterprise's logistics on an ongoing basis and to recommend measures aimed at improving the logistics processes functioning in the enterprise. Moreover, a successful logistics audit is inextricably linked to understanding the key stakeholders (including suppliers, business partners, customers, and local authorities) who directly or indirectly affect the logistics of the enterprise in general and its logistics system in particular. This means that, in practice, the requirements for auditors dealing with logistics audit should be, above all, good knowledge of issues related to broadly understood logistics, supply chain and logistics systems, as well as (preferably) several years of experience working in the logistics industry. Thus, in the opinion of the authors, this requirement should not be fulfilled by an auditor who has experience in the implementation of industry audits but not in those directly related to logistics; especially since industry audits, in comparison with, for example, financial audits, are characterized by a much higher degree of complexity, and thus of various problems. Each logistics audit should, therefore, be strictly tailored to the specific needs and requirements of each organization, and its initiation should be preceded by a thorough analysis and good preparation in the areas of:

- logistics audit planning – the plan and activities related to the implementation of the audit should be prepared in accordance with applicable standards and well in advance,
- research and critical analysis of existing data – auditors should have at their disposal relevant data, of high quality, coming from the organization (including its systems, processes, procedures, or from the employees themselves), which should then be subjected to detailed analysis. Only data prepared in this way should be compiled and compared with the adopted criteria and standards in order to formulate final conclusions and issue recommendations,
- communication – the results of the logistics audit should be clearly communicated to people who are directly and indirectly interested in

it. On the other hand, reporting methods, including post-audit reports, must comply with the applicable standards issued by the IIA,
● monitoring – logistics auditors should observe and control the functioning of the enterprise's logistics system or its supply chain on an ongoing basis in order to take corrective actions resulting from the completed logistics audit.

The next stage of preparatory work as part of the implementation of a logistics audit should include activities related to the construction and understanding of the logistics system model functioning within the analyzed enterprise. In practice this centers on (Gattorna et al., 1991):

a. defining the logistics goals of the enterprise in the context of broader corporate and marketing goals,
b. determining the target level of service provision and other logistics activities and products,
c. identifying flowcharts regarding communication in the execution of orders from customers,
d. identifying flowcharts of material flows and the corresponding data and information flows,
e. determining the places where there are discrepancies and overlapping flows of physical goods or information,
f. defining important interdependencies between the logistics function and other areas of activity.

Thanks to the analysis and graphical approach to the logistics system, the auditor will be able to know to what extent the processes existing within a given model achieve the goal assigned to them.

With knowledge of what prompts enterprises to conduct logistics audits and what actions, and in which areas these must be taken in this regard, we can now proceed to describe the basic stages of logistics audit implementation (see Table 2.3). The first stage focuses on the comprehensive preparation of the logistics audit and determining the principles under which it will be carried out. In practice, this is a series of activities that focus on determining the needs of the organization in the field of logistics audit, appointing a team of auditors (or auditor) and appointing the lead auditor (team leader), defining the main processes and those supporting the implementation of the enterprise's operational and strategic goals, determining the scope and scale of management involvement in the audit process, developing research areas, and informing employees about the date and rules for the implementation of audit activities. Often, the quality of the implementation of tasks resulting from the first stage of the logistics

Table 2.3 Basic stages of logistics audit implementation

Stages of logistics audit	Tasks
Stage I: Preparation of a holistic logistics audit concept	1.1. Prerequisites and motivation for conducting a logistic audit 1.2. Definition of the general objective and sub-objectives of the audit 1.3. Selection of auditors and possibly conclusion of an agreement with the entity 1.4. Involvement of management and use of their potential 1.5. Definition of the scope of the tests 1.6. Informing employees about the implementation of the audit
Stage II: Implementation of pre-audit actions	2.1. Development of an auditorium survey 2.2. Preparation of the audit plan and program 2.3. Conducting preliminary research by means of an auditorium-based survey 2.4. Analysis of the auditorium survey – obtaining information *vs.* inference 2.5. Preparation of pre-audit reports 2.6. Organization of an information meeting
Stage III: Implementation of the audit	3.1. Adoption of criteria for the evaluation of the studied area, unit, department, etc. 3.2. Determination of the actual state of logistics activities 3.3. Determination of the state of declared logistics activity 3.4. Comparative analysis of factual and declared facts 3.5. Inference 3.6. Indication of improvement activities (corrections, advice, recommendations)
Stage IV: Implementation of post-audit actions	4.1. Assessment of the course of audit activities as part of the audit 4.2. Evaluation of the correctness and quality of the data collected 4.3. Preparation of audit results 4.4. Recommendations for further audit activities in the areas concerned 4.5. Monitoring of improvement activities 4.6. Organizing the closing meeting

Source: Authors' own study.

audit has a significant impact on the others. Thus, the auditor should treat with particular care issues related to informing employees about the implementation of the logistics audit, because its efficiency and effectiveness will depend on their attitude, commitment, and emotional approach. The second stage, in contrast to the first, is already associated with the need to carry out pre-audit tasks, i.e., those immediately preceding the implementation of the proper audit. They include preparation of an audit survey, an audit plan and program, conducting preliminary individual and group surveys by means of a questionnaire, analysis and development of conclusions from the conducted research, and informing the management of the entity about the results of pre-audit activities. The third stage of the logistics audit is extremely important, because it is here that the actual state of logistics activity is determined and compared with the declared state. It is at this stage that not only the enterprise, but above all the management team, which is responsible for its development, is informally evaluated for its previous work. The final product of this stage of logistics audit comes in the form of conclusions, corrections, and recommendations, which are then included in post-audit reports, which are the foundation of each audit's documentation. The fourth stage is the final one and in fact boils down to assessing both the course of audit activities and the correctness of the collected data and presenting the final results of the audit. At this stage, the auditor also formulates recommendations as to the need to undertake audit work in other areas of the organization in the future. A kind of overarching mechanism connecting the entire program and conduct of the logistics audit is the organization of the closing meeting, which is a holistic summary of the work related to the audit carried out in the enterprise. Table 2.3 presents a detailed list of tasks that are carried out at individual stages of the logistics audit.

In order to supplement knowledge about the stages of logistics audit, a block diagram of its implementation in graphic terms is presented (see Figure 2.2), which is to contribute to its better consolidation.

The logistics audit is increasingly being considered as an important tool for improving processes taking place in organizations because it takes up important topics from the point of view of the organization's management, concerned with assessing the quality of logistics operations, the level of productivity of logistics systems, or the effectiveness of managing relationships with customers and suppliers. Thanks to its use, management staff can make a deeper diagnosis of problem areas, for example by quickly identifying key deviations that may occur both within the existing logistics infrastructure, logistics organization, logistics system, supply chain, or ICT infrastructure. In this context, the question arises when and under what circumstances the enterprise management should use a logistics audit[8] and what measurable benefits it can bring him. The answer to this question is neither simple nor unambiguous, especially considering the set of specific features and problems that characterize each organization. However, while making a certain generalization, it can be said that the basic premises for implementing a logistics audit in an enterprise should be:

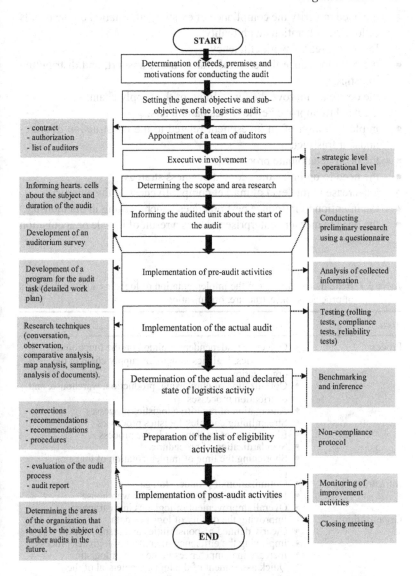

Figure 2.2 Logistics audit procedure – graphic design Source: Authors' own study.

- the need to verify the compliance of existing information on the results of logistics operations with reality,
- low or decreased work efficiency,
- the need to reduce the costs of warehouse, transport, and distribution logistics,
- the desire to improve the functioning of the supply chain,
- the need to improve key logistics parameters,
- implementation of an investment related to the construction of warehouse infrastructure,
- the need to automate processes,
- the need to optimize the adopted business strategy,
- a decrease in the level of market competitiveness of the enterprise,
- the intention to introduce best practices/benchmarking in the industry,[9]
- the need to measure enterprise value as a result of its sale or acquisition (merger).

Table 2.4 Benefits resulting from the implementation of logistics audit in the areas of processes, infrastructure, organization

Area	Benefits
Process	• Objective (independent) opinion on the functioning of logistics, logistics system, or supply chain in the organization • Optimization of purchasing, production, warehouse, and distribution processes • Automation of repetitive logistics processes • Streamlining complex logistics processes • Elimination of bottlenecks in the process • Standardization of procedures • Shortening the time of implementation of logistics processes
Infrastructure	• Optimization of product storage • Increasing safety processes in the warehouse • Overall improvement of logistics infrastructure
Organization	• Improving the quality of logistics data • Clearly defined responsibilities and responsibilities • Improving the efficiency of control of logistics processes • Increase in competences in the area of logistics • Quick assessment of the logistic potential of the organization by comparing with the best models • Estimation of the costs of logistics processes • Cost reduction • Reduction of risks related to the functioning of the organization • Reducing the burden of managing the entire organization • Increase in the return on assets

Source: Authors' own study.

As for the benefits that the enterprise can gain – incidentally on many levels – thanks to the use of an auxiliary tool in the form of a logistics audit, their list is significant and is presented in detail below in Table 2.4. On this basis, we can also conclude that the greatest asset for an enterprise using this type of audit is the ability to improve (enhance/perfect) the logistics system by identifying ineffective activities and agreeing on directions of improvement of processes, procedures, and systems in a specific area of the organization. As a consequence, there is both a reduction in the costs of logistics activities and an increase in the quality of services provided.

2.4. Problem areas of the logistics audit

According to Kaczmarek (2016), each organization is always characterized by a certain "organized complexity" and a system of interconnected subsystems, the functioning and cooperation of which determine its existence and development. Since the organization remains in constant interactions, often multidimensional and dynamic, with its environment, it is natural that they can be a source of support and help, as well as obstacles or problems. In practice, in the process of managing the organization management staff constantly encounter some difficulties or dysfunctions, due to – holistically speaking – the permanent failure of the organization to adapt to the rapidly changing world, the matter of which is as interesting as it is unpredictable. Therefore, it can be concluded that problems are in fact an immanent feature of the functioning of any organization and a natural everyday reality for its managers.

At the beginning of the considerations on the problem areas of logistics audit, it is worth making a few remarks about the essence of the very concept of the problem, which – and this is worth emphasizing – in management science has received many interpretations, but not always ones enriching its content or essence. Nevertheless, the problem is most often understood as a difficulty that can take on a theoretical or practical character, and that causes an inquisitive attitude, leading ultimately to enrichment of knowledge (Kupisiewicz, 1964). A more comprehensive approach to the term is proposed by Nosal (1993), who believes that the problem becomes everything that raises our – even the slightest – doubt, causes discrepancies between the actual and expected state, and hinders the possibility of solving the task using available knowledge and developed methods (formulas). The concept is defined slightly differently by Linhart (1976), who believes that the problem is in practice an interactive relationship between the subject and its environment, having the features of internal conflict, which the subject tries to solve by seeking to move from the initial state to the final state (goal). According to Linhart, it is the existence of the problem itself that is in fact the source of motivation for the subject to solve it. At the same time, as he quickly adds, in order to solve a specific problem, the entity must look for new and often non-standard solutions that will go beyond the previously adopted framework. This is also associated with the need to search for new sources of knowledge and information on effective ways of solving problems or, more broadly, problem situations. Thus, summarizing the content contained in the above definitions of the word problem, we can conventionally assume that it is any situation (quantified or not) that requires a solution by a person or a group of people, using both standard and non-standard (read: new) means (patterns, tools, techniques, etc.). On the basis of science – including management science – problems can take both different forms, can be subject to non-uniform criteria of division, and be the subject of a wide range of research. Detailed information on this subject is included in Table 2.5, which comprehensively presents the types of problems faced by researchers, who undertake scientific research in various fields of knowledge and science.

Understanding the word problem – including its types, divisions, and references – means that we can now move on to discuss another, closely related issue concerning the "problem area." The answer to the question "what is a problem area," is neither easy nor unambiguous. This situation is caused by interpretative considerations, because the term itself in the literature of management science has been explained many times. Apart from this thread, however, we can assume that we will consider as problem areas in management those organizational and technical spheres of enterprise functioning that are the source of anomalies and deviations. Moreover, eliminating problem areas requires the involvement of forces and resources that may come from within the organization and/or from its external environment. At this point, it should be emphasized that in studies – not only those of a scientific nature – the term "problem area" is often used interchangeably with such terms as difficult areas, conflict areas, danger areas, areas of deviation, or – in general – research areas. However, the use of the term "research areas" seems to be the most appropriate, i.e., the closest to the term "problem areas," because from the point of view of the theory of logic, the solution of any conflict or problem should be preceded by a thorough analysis of its nature, and thus be well studied. Thus, problem areas are defined within various fields of science, scientific disciplines, or specialties. The result of this is scientific research conducted e.g., on problem areas in Poland, in the aspect of the objectives of the Regional Policy of the European Union (EU), problem areas of project management, or identification of problem areas in supply-chain management. Problem areas are also identified and then investigated as part of a logistics audit. Their distinction also requires the use of the right approach (diagnostic approach, prognostic

Table 2.5 Types of research problems – characteristics

Division criterion	Type of problem	Characteristics of the problem	Author/Source
Nature of the problem	Deviation problems	Problems related to the formation of various types of defects in the organization, the causes of which are not known to us. In order to eliminate these deviations, it is necessary to conduct studies that will determine their cause. However, the information collected during the research is to prevent the emergence of such problems in the future	Penc, 2007
	Optimization problems	Problems that arise as a result of the need to introduce adaptive changes in the current functioning of the organization, due to changes taking place in its closer and further environment. It is about improving management methods, processes, techniques, functions, tools, systems, logistics, information flow, etc., in order to improve the efficiency of the entire organization	
	Innovative problems	Problems resulting from creative changes taking place both in the organization and in its environment. Nowadays, innovation is seen as an important element of the organization's offensive strategy, especially those organizations entering new markets, as well as a defensive weapon for those that already have a stable market position and a good reputation	
Degree of structuring	Well-structured problems	Problems whose structure is well known to us mainly in quantitative terms. These problems can be quantified because they have been well recognized, and mathematical models and precise measurement tools have been developed to solve them	Antoszkiewicz, 1999

(*Continued*)

Table 2.5 (Continued)

Division criterion	Type of problem	Characteristics of the problem	Author/Source
	Poorly structured problems	Problems with a poorly defined structure. They contain both qualitative and quantitative elements. At the same time, the quality elements are the ones that stand out	
	Unstructured problems	Problems with an indefinite structure. They can be defined only qualitatively – in verbal form – due to the lack of quantitative relationships between the elements. These kinds of problems can be described, but they cannot be measured	
Complexity	Simple problems	Basic problems, usually the relationships between the elements of the problem are linear, so specific causes give rise to specific effects	Own elaboration
	Compound problems	Problems that are bigger than simple problems, usually the relationships between the elements of the problem are non-linear and can take on different forms or forms	
	Complex problems	Highly complex problems, often involving larger parts of the organization. These are problems whose effects are difficult to predict and their occurrence can give rise to a domino effect	
	Chaos problems	Crisis-based problems. Requiring quick intervention and action on the part of management	
Creation status	Problems related to the improvement of the existing state	These are problems regarding deviations and optimizations. The starting point for solving them is to determine the facts	Bielińska-Dusza, 2009
	Problems with creating a new organization	Problems related to the implementation of forecasts and long-term plans	

Source: Authors' own study.

approach), selection of appropriate indicators (quantitative, qualitative), adoption of specific measurement scales (nominal scale, ordinal scale, interval scale, quotient scale), and the use of the appropriate inference scheme (deductive inference, inductive inference). To sum up, we can see that the proper diagnosis of a problem area requires not only knowledge and experience within a given sector or industry but also the ability to apply appropriate measurement techniques. Only then can the areas designated in this way be called problem areas. Taking into account the above, Lisiński (2011) distinguishes three basic groups of research problems as part of a logistics audit:

- first group – this involves the assessment of the appropriateness of the logistics strategy adopted by the organization to the strategy of the enterprise itself and the review and evaluation of the process of defining the logistics strategy,
- second group – this concerns the analysis and evaluation of solutions in the area of logistics organization, the location of logistics tasks in the organizational structure of the enterprise, and the ways of performing logistics functions,
- third group – this refers directly to the research and analysis of logistics processes taking place in the organization, and related to production logistics, supply logistics, distribution logistics, waste logistics, storage, transport, inventory, or IT systems.

It should be noted that the main problem (research) areas of logistics audit (see Bielińska-Dusza, 2009) presented by Lisiński (2011) in fact correspond to the basic areas of activity of each organization, concerning strategy, structure, and processes. In the case of processes, Table 2.6 below, presents – in an exhaustive manner – the characteristics of problem areas that are most often subjected to research and analysis as part of the implementation of tasks in the field of logistics audit. Thus, from the scale of effective identification of errors, deviations, anomalies, and irregularities in these areas (see Table 2.6), we will be able to talk about either healthy or pathological features of the system related to the functioning of the logistics system within a given enterprise.

2.5. Logistics audit in the era of Industry 4.0

There is no denying that, in fact, since the dawn of time, technological breakthroughs have brought about, and continue to do so, fundamental changes in economies and societies in almost every respect. In general, they

Table 2.6 Typology of problem areas of logistics audit

Area	Characteristics
Warehouse management	Its aim is to improve operational activities and optimize the use of warehouse equipment, organize and monitor the storage process, analyze goods and information flows in the storage process, and identify key problems of warehouse management
Inventory management	It covers the structure of inventories, their rotation coverage rate, the process of replenishment of stock, and directions of improvement
Order fulfillment	It concerns the structure of orders, the assessment of the costs of handling complaints and returns, as well as the examination of the level of handling complaints and returns and the actual level of customer service
Transport	It is related to the implementation of activities in the area of transport, the correctness of the selection of rolling stock, the efficiency of its use, the choice between own and foreign transport, rolling stock management, indicating the directions of improvements in this area
Logistic information systems	It includes analysis and assessment of the degree of implementation of information systems, determination of the use of individual information channels, analysis of document circulation, determination of network architecture, tests of existing hardware security, verification of the effectiveness of systems, ensuring security of access to systems
Packaging and recyclable resources	Diagnosis of packaging burdened with the obligation of recovery, determination of the method of their recording, the optimal way to ensure the required levels of recovery and recycling
Distribution system	It includes audits in the areas of warehousing, inventory management, transportation and order fulfillment, network configuration, freight flows, distribution organization and improvement directions
Production system	It involves a reliable assessment of production logistics and setting priorities enabling the right and effective decisions related to it; besides, it allows you to improve operational activities and optimize the use of the enterprise's production infrastructure. It covers all aspects of production, from planning sales cycles, through storage and supply of raw materials, flows on production halls, to production reporting with its marking
Supply system	It is subordinated to the review of the status of the procedures of the purchasing department and the verification of commercial contracts. This includes analysis of the ordering system, suppliers and prices, verification of contracts and preliminary preparation for negotiations with suppliers, as well as analysis and structure of inventory

(Continued)

Table 2.6 (Continued)

Area	Characteristics
Supply chain	It allows, among other things, the identification of the strengths and weaknesses of the chain and the processes implemented in it, analysis of the current configuration of the supply chain and the infrastructure used, and assessment of the relationship between the links
Cross-docking*	It allows for reducing total costs in the supply chain, thanks to the fact that the goods are not stored. However, the effective and effective use of cross-docking requires precise synchronization of processes related to the receipt and release of goods
Automation of logistics processes*	It concerns the implementation of a comprehensive solution that will integrate human resources, material resources (machines), and advanced IT systems. It can cover all areas of logistics audit. The scale of process automation should be economically justified and take into account the permissible level of errors in processes, the exceeding of which gives rise to significant levels of risk for the organization

Source: (Żebrucki, 2012, p. 427).
* Typology supplemented with areas added by the authors of the study.

take the form of technical, economic, and social transformations, which significantly transform the current picture of the functioning of the world both qualitatively and quantitatively. It is common to call such phenomena industrial revolutions[10] or, less frequently, industrial overthrows. The term Industrial Revolution was used for the first time at the end of the 18th century to describe the mechanization of production with the participation of steam and water (steam age), which gave rise to mechanical production systems. Then came the Second Industrial Revolution (at the end of the 19th century and the beginning of the 20th), which resulted in the construction of the world's first assembly line at the Ford automotive plant (in 1913). Subsequently, the key issues for the Second Industrial Revolution in the form of standardization and mechanization of production evolved toward its coordination and automation, which formed, in turn, the Third Industrial Revolution (1970s). However, in relation to its predecessors, it was already characterized by a high degree of automation of industrial production (the era of industrial automation), which, incidentally, was the result of the use of advanced information and communication systems. Nowadays, we are already dealing with the Fourth Industrial Revolution, the creation of which would not have been possible without the participation of advanced technology, in the form of the Internet. To a level previously unknown, it revolutionized the level of innovation of products, services, systems, or technologies available on the market. The latter have evolved from the digital level to the level of artificial intelligence (AI)[11] and machine learning (ML).[12] Moreover, the scope of the Fourth Industrial Revolution is much more extensive and much more profound than it was in earlier such phenomena (Buła & Niedzielski, 2021). Currently, not only based on theory but also practice, we use the term "Industry 4.0" much more often – referring to the current industrial revolution – rather than the "fourth industrial revolution." Nevertheless, both these terms function in public space as synonyms[13] and are therefore used interchangeably. Industry 4.0 – as a conceptual category – has functioned in the world of science and business since 2011 thanks to the annual industrial trade show Hannover Messe. The use of the phrase "Industry 4.0" was directly related to the concept of "Industrie 4.0," promoted by the representatives of the German business, political, and scientific world in favor of strengthening the competitiveness of German industry, in the face of quickly catching up on competition from China. As a result, the development of Industry 4.0 has become a key element in Germany's new research and technological innovation policy. This idea was rapidly taken up by the governments of other countries, especially those that want to maintain their good market position on the map of global competitiveness. As for the objectives that guide the idea of Industry 4.0, they relate primarily to (Hochmuth et al., 2017):

1) At the level of strategy:
   a) building new business models and services using digital products,
   b) shortening the time of introducing new products to the market, in response to rapidly changing customer requirements,
   c) increasing the degree of resistance of the organization to changing customer tastes,
2) At the level of the organization:
   a) improving the quality of work by better reconciling professional and private duties,
   b) automation of routine tasks,
   c) creating a user-oriented work environment thanks to innovative human–machine interaction,
3) At process level:
   a) time savings due to more efficient and transparent production processes,
   b) increasing the flexibility of processes through dynamic planning, control, and execution,
   c) increase productivity and save resources for customized products,
   d) shortening the time of process implementation using intelligent analyses,

e) diversification of work organization through mobile control and execution processes,
f) increase quality by predictively avoiding errors,
g) increase the efficiency of processes using technology in the areas of data collection, data transfer, and data analysis.

In the context of the above-mentioned objectives, therefore, the question arises: what are they supposed to serve? The answer – which may be surprising – is not difficult, because in the era of Industry 4.0, a completely new model of organization (enterprises, factories) will be developed, which – unlike its predecessors – will be "smarter" (see Table 2.7). The combination of the adjective "intelligent" with the noun "factory" is by no means accidental, because the point is that the newly formed type of organization should act similarly to a thinking being and adapt its functioning to the changing environment through appropriate adaptation of the most modern solutions and technologies.

In practice, smart factories are therefore to become enterprises based on cyber-physical systems and linking them with the use of the Internet of Things in industry and organization of production.[14] The structure that will connect all the devices, sensors, systems, and machines in the enterprise will cause production losses, malfunctions, and downtime to disappear. In addition, goods produced in smart factories will be characterized by a high level of customization, and production processes will be characterized by a high level of digitization.

Highly advanced technology related to Industry 4.0 (including the Internet of Things, Internet of Services, cyber-physical systems) will therefore also significantly determine the future shape, "appearance," and structure of the internal audit, which is already referred to as the "fourth generation internal audit" (Internal Audit 4.0, IA 4.0). Its final face is not yet known to us, but there is no doubt that Internal Audit 4.0 (like Logistics Audit 4.0) will be a process of objective acquisition of data from the Internet, cyber-physical systems, and factories of the future, which, subjected to analysis and model visualization, will identify patterns, anomalies, or deviations from the desired state. Thanks to this, internal auditors will be able to carry out the tasks they face more effectively than before, which in practice will bring enterprises closer to achieving their goals at both the operational and strategic levels. There is no doubt that smart factories will need a "smart" audit that is tailored to their structures, tools, processes, and strategies. Thus, it can be expected that auditing as we know it today will evolve toward digital audit (see Table 2.8) – this also applies to industry audits, including logistics audit – mainly due to the undeniable fact that the world itself is becoming more digital (for more on this, see Section 1.3)

Table 2.7 Modern enterprise vs. future enterprise – similarities and differences

Item	Data Source	Contemporary enterprise		The enterprise of the future	
		Features	*Technology*	*Features*	*Technology*
Tool	Sensor	Precision	Intelligent sensors and fault detection	Self-awareness, self-assessment	Monitoring degradation, predicting the remaining service life
Machine	Controller	Efficiency, productivity	Monitoring and diagnostics of equipment operating conditions	Self-awareness, self-assessment, self-resistance	Uptime with predictive "health" monitoring
Production system	Network system	Productivity and overall equipment efficiency	Cost-effective operations: reduction of labor and waste	Self-employment, self-configuration, self-organization	Hassle-free productivity

Source: Lee et al. (2015).

Table 2.8 Changes taking place in internal audit

Area	Historical	Contemporary	Innovative
Purpose	Audit of units carried out on a rotational basis, on the basis of an approved plan	Audit of units carried out on the basis of defined risk areas	Audit of units based on strategic, operational and business risk
Perspective	Historical	Historical	Future-oriented
Style	Corporate	Patriarchal	Consultative, advisory, and expert
Authorization	Compliance with policies and procedures	Ensuring financial control: compliance	Business compliance
Focus on risk	Financial	Financial	Corporate
Toolbox	Abacus, calculators	IT programs to provide control for key processes	Highly advanced digital tools using artificial intelligence and machine-learning technology
Technology	Basic office supplies	Automated working documents	Digital testing and continuous monitoring

Source: Authors' own study based on (Norman, 2009, p. 10).

This situation is likely to herald a turnaround in the internal audit over the next few years, due to the rapid digitization of enterprises and institutions. Its scope will cover almost the entire methodology of conducting internal audit, including, in particular, audit tools and techniques. The changes will concern in particular:

- The method of collecting, preparing, and analyzing data – at this point it should be mentioned that thanks to such technologies as cloud computing, big data, the Internet of Things (IoT), etc., it will be possible to access data (information) in real time from anywhere in the world. This means that auditors will not have to – as has been the case so far – waste a lot of time gaining access to these technologies, which has often been difficult for reasons such as logistics. In addition, the entire process related to the processing of audit data will be digitized, which means that basic and even advanced audit tasks in applications or data sources will no longer require human intervention, but only supervision. Technologically advanced solutions will also allow auditors to

extract the right information even from those data sets that are not structured (e.g., images, sounds, videos, posts, text files, emails). What's
more, the new solutions will allow for better identification of risk in the
organization, using tools that will combine elements of statistics, data
visualization, data and process mining, artificial intelligence, machine
learning, or algorithmics,

- control and security of information in various areas of the organization
  – due to the fact that digital data are most often stored in IT systems or
  databases, access to them will be granted and supervised by machines
  based on algorithms. In practice, this is to prevent an attempt to misuse
  them by unauthorized persons,
- The basic scope of knowledge, competences, and skills – because organizations, and thus internal audit, will undergo far-reaching digitization,
  it will be necessary to supplement the specialist knowledge in the audit
  with new elements, related to, for example, computer science or algorithmics. Nevertheless, the human factor will remain the most important value for the enterprise, as the ultimate guarantor of the validity
  and quality of the audit process in both holistic and fragmented terms.
  However, in the case of competences and skills, cognitive abilities[15] and
  meta-skills[16] will play a special role among auditors and employees.

2.6. Control and analytical questions

Control questions

1. Give a definition and briefly characterize the logistics system of the
   enterprise.
2. Give a definition – broadly and narrowly – of a logistics audit.
3. Present the basic goals that a logistics audit has to achieve.
4. The areas subject to logistic audit in storage and production processes
   are …?
5. Complete the basic stages – along with the tasks assigned to them – of
   the logistics audit.
6. Present in a graphical terms the procedure for the course of a logistics
   audit.
7. Describe the benefits of a logistics audit in the areas of processes and
   organizations.
8. Characterize the problem area of logistics audit in relation to warehouse management, production systems, and automation of logistics
   processes.
9. According to Lisiński (2011), as part of the logistics audit, there are
   three basic groups of research problems. What are they?

10. Describe the changes taking place in the internal audit, taking into account the area related to the purpose of the audit, the style, and the technology used.

Analytical questions

1. In the opinion of Jezierski (2007a), industry audits are a tool used to assess the activities of management and individual decision-making links of the organization, and their main task is to provide information necessary for continuous improvement of processes and systems related to the functioning of a given area and/or organizational unit within a given enterprise. With that in mind, do you agree that industry audits will continue to grow in popularity over the next few years? Justify your opinion.
2. Since the logistics audit is a voluntary audit and therefore carried out at the request of the ordering party, under what circumstances would you recommend – to the management of the organization – its conduct?
3. What benefits and disadvantages do you see from the implementation of a logistics audit at the strategic and operational level of the organization?
4. On the basis of science and practice, the phrase "the world in which we live is becoming more and more digital" is more and more often repeated. In your opinion, does this mean that logistics auditing is also becoming more and more a digital audit? Give your opinion on this topic using practical examples.
5. Describe possible scenarios for the development of logistics audit in the context of Industry 4.0.

Notes

1 The founder of general systems theory is considered to be the Austrian biologist and philosopher Ludwig von Bertalanffy, who interpreted the system as a whole consisting of parts remaining in a state of interaction. For more information, see Von Bertalanffy, L. (1984). *General Systems Theory: Basics, Development, Applications*, PWN, Warsaw.
2 Nevertheless, we should be aware that the concept of a system is defined differently depending on the area in which it is applied. Therefore, in the opinion of Szklarski and Kozioł (1980), it can take on different meanings and, in technology, the system is understood as assigning to a specific purpose the operation of a set of objects interconnected with each other; in organization and planning, the system is understood as a set of time-related operations; in scientific and research work, the system is understood as the field of general methodology for the study of processes and phenomena related to any area of human activity;

while in the field of cognitive theory, the system means a certain method of scientific thinking in the process of solving complex control tasks.

3 For more information, see https://www.elalog.eu/.

4 According to Gołembska (2010) elements of the logistics system are material and human resources, as well as source data and information that can be separated into homogeneous logistics subsystems, are fully reflected in the enterprise's financial documentation, and are a quantitatively and quantitatively record of the volume and structure of demand for products or services.

5 This is the active management of supply-chain activities that aims to maximize customer value and achieve a sustainable competitive advantage. In practice, this induces enterprises to run and develop your supply chains in the most efficient way. Activities in this area include product development, procurement, production, distribution, and IT systems, which are currently necessary to coordinate these activities.

6 For more on the impact of megatrends on the global economy and societies, see Naisbitt, J. (1997). *Megatrends: Ten New Directions Changing Our Lives.* Zysk i S-ka Wydawnictwo, Poznań.

7 An example of a narrow approach to the definition of logistics audit can be that proposed by Sungurtekin (2011), for whom a logistics audit is an activity that always begins with the collection of quantitative and qualitative data from key stakeholders of the organization and their analysis and interpretation. On the other hand, the main units cooperating and participating in the collection of this data and conducting interviews are most often the following departments: logistics, transport, warehouse, purchasing, production, trade, customer service, or IT. All of them are directly or indirectly involved in the supply chain and can provide valuable insights into the situation and benefit from the results and conclusions contained in the documentation post-auction.

8 A logistics audit is a voluntary audit. This means that it is carried out at the request of the ordering party and it is not the result of the law.

9 The process of improvement, consisting of the use of experience and the best global models and practices that are implemented for the needs of the organization.

10 It is widely believed that we can talk about an industrial revolution when there is a significant increase in the efficiency of production systems, which is the result of the use of new technology.

11 Artificial intelligence is, in fact, a specific type of system that can rationally solve multidimensional problems or take actions to achieve previously set goals. The term "artificial intelligence" was first used in 1955 by the eminent mathematician and computer scientist John McCarthy.

12 Machine learning is an area of artificial intelligence concerning algorithms that participate in the process of self-improvement through their experience. In other words, it is a process in which the computer learns something new on its own, based on algorithms and collected data.

13 There are also other synonyms for the term "Industry 4.0" in the literature, including Industry of the Future, The Cyber-Physical System Era (CPSs Era), Production of the Future, Intelligent manufacturing systems (IMSs), and 4IR (Fourth Industrial Revolution). In Anglo-Saxon countries, the term "Internet of Things" is also used, as is the "Internet of Everything" (IoE) and the "Industrial Internet of Things" (IIoT).

14 This is a prediction by specialists (Robinson, J. (2014). *Smart Factory and the Internet of The Things Opportunity*. https://blogs.intel.com/) who claim that by 2025, 80 to 100 percent of production may already be using applications for Internet stuff. This means that machines, sensors, and other devices will connect to each other and communicate via the Internet.

15 Cognitive abilities include thinking, speech, evaluating, understanding, data processing, and spatial orientation.

16 These are abilities that allow an individual to function effectively in a rapidly changing reality or environment.

3 Logistics audit

A modular approach

3.1. Logistics audit of procurement

Synchronization and communication of processes related to materials management are among the most difficult activities that logisticians have to perform in order for the supply subsystem in the enterprise's logistics system to function properly. In terms of definition, materials management concerns those spheres of economic activity that cover all phenomena and processes related to the management of materials[1] (raw materials, semi-finished products) at all levels of management (Statistics Poland, 2020). The processes taking place in the area of materials management include those that relate to the acquisition, supply, and use of materials in all phases of the economic process and their movement (delivery). A complementary – although slightly different – view of the essence of material management in the enterprise is presented by J. Arnold et al. (2008), who claim that it performs a coordinating function both in terms of planning and of controlling the flow of materials in the organization. At the same time, they point to the implementation of two basic goals, which are reduced to:

- maximizing the use of the limited resources of the organization,
- providing the required level of customer service.

Let us note that the objectives presented within the framework of material management, although they are equivalent to each other, nevertheless contain a certain element of antinomicity. In practice, it is not easy to provide customers with what they want, taking into account the limitations that often result from time and space, while maintaining low costs. And this means that materials management must be a compromise between the level of customer service and the cost of services provided to them. Especially since these costs increase in direct proportion to the level and quality of what is offered. Due to this, alternative solutions are constantly

DOI: 10.4324/9781003380184-4

being sought based on practice, which, thanks to the potential savings made in various areas of the enterprise's operations, will compensate for the costs it incurs in the field of customer service. Thus, one should agree with the thesis put forward by Arnold et al. (2008) that the general problem of materials management is that of maintaining a balance between priority and efficiency. In the context of materials management, the priority for the organization still remains the importance with which it approaches production planning in relation to market demand, which is determined by the volume of demand. In the case of efficiency, it is primarily about the most effective functioning of the organization's operating system, which will be a determinant in the context of the volume of production or goods delivered to the market. Both the first and the second conceptual categories referred to here must be subject to constant verification and control in order to be able to effectively meet the requirements set for them by customers who constantly demand better prices and higher quality of service. These challenges must be faced by materials management on a daily basis. Nowadays – especially in the field of logistics – next to materials management, the element that can ultimately determine the success or failure of the enterprise is procurement. According to Słowiński (2008), it is a concept that has a broader meaning than purchasing,[2] and should be understood as a process of acquiring goods and services. As he quickly adds, procurement is a process that deliberately connects the participants in the supply chain and guarantees the right quality that is provided by the suppliers in this chain. The cardinal task of a well-functioning procurement process is to ensure that the raw materials and semi-finished products necessary in the production process are delivered when they are needed. In addition, the enterprise's logistics system has several other tasks to fulfill (Lysons, 2004):

- the purchase of materials necessary for production on the basis of its plan,
- the organization of the flow of information and financial resources regarding the purchase of materials,
- verifying that the material in question is of sufficiently good quality,
- identification of new suppliers and establishing close cooperation with them,
- negotiating prices from suppliers and conditions for the purchase of raw materials,
- control of deliveries,
- finalizing deliveries,
- receipt and storage of deliveries,
- maintaining a low (optimal) level of stocks,

- close integration and cooperation with departments using the purchased materials, taking into account understanding their needs and obtaining materials at the right time.

In relation to the tasks described above, that are to be accomplished by the sphere of procurement in the functioning of the enterprise, it should be emphasized only that its economic effectiveness – in a holistic approach – will not be determined only by the fact of obtaining raw materials for production at the lowest possible price but by the synergy effect that it can achieve from cooperation in the implementation of each of the tasks. The last element, next to materials management and procurement, which in the context of a logistics audit of procurement needs to be discussed, is the so-called procurement logistics. In terms of the explanatory approach, procurement logistics is a process that determines the distribution, condition, and flows of materials in an enterprise and requires constant coordination (Krawczyk, 2000). As noted by Skuza (2019), its main role is to prevent a situation in which production could be interrupted. Therefore, it must effectively and economically meet all the materials needs that the enterprise has. In practice, this boils down to the fact that procurement logistics must simultaneously ensure the expected completeness, reliability, and quality of deliveries on the one hand, and guarantee their timeliness, flexibility, and speed on the other. Any disturbances in this area may hinder, or even prevent, the proper functioning of the entire logistics system of the enterprise. This is because the system is characterized by a high degree of consistency, which consequently leads to a situation where changes made within one subsystem mechanically imply those occurring in others. As Mroczko (2016) emphasizes, procurement logistics is therefore a complicated process, especially since it must strive to minimize the costs associated with the purchase and maintenance of inventory, as well as to maintain their high quality. What seems to distinguish procurement logistics from other elements of the enterprise's logistics system is that it is strongly connected with the market because all the materials necessary to secure the production process come from the market. Thus, it is a key link in the supply chain of any enterprise. In synthetic terms, the main goal that procurement logistics has to achieve is considered to be (Kowalczyk, 2015):

- obtaining from the market and preparing materials for production,
- organizing an efficient flow of materials and information assigned to it.

Its implementation is the result of tasks and activities, which in graphic terms are presented in Figure 3.1.

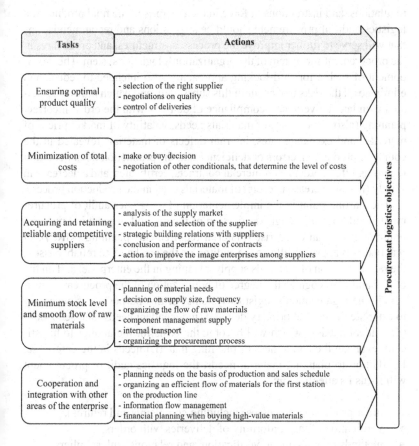

Figure 3.1 Procurement logistics objectives divided into tasks and activities Source: Authors' own study on the basis of Abt (1998).

Materials management, procurement, and procurement logistics are key issues, knowledge of which in both theoretical and practical contexts seems to be a *sine qua non* for a proper understanding of the nature of the logistics audit of procurement; especially since the concept itself in this form is quite rarely used and therefore little known, which is also confirmed in the literature devoted to audit issues, including internal or industry audit. Therefore, when attempting to define the logistics audit of procurement, we can conclude that it is a tool for regular review of logistics activities in the area of procurement, whose task is to assess the compliance of the state of implementation of processes related to the planning of materials needs, selection of suppliers, and organization of supply supplies with the procedures, regulations, and instructions in force in the enterprise. The final product of a logistics audit of procurement should be suggestions and recommendations that will serve to further improve the processes, structures, and procedures in the procurement subsystem of the organization's logistics system. The development of such a forward-looking approach is also intended to reduce and eliminate all the risks that occur in this subsystem, and which may be associated with late delivery, non-compliance of delivery with the order, incorrect planning (also forecasting) of materials needs, volatility of market prices of materials and exchange rates, internal defects of materials revealed in the course of production, errors or deficiencies in the production documentation regarding offers, orders, commercial contracts, certificates, and a decrease in supply (i.e., an increase in costs) of materials used in the production process.

The starting point in the implementation of a logistics audit of procurement should be a thorough verification of the method of planning material requirements in an enterprise (material requirements planning (MRP)). In practice, this approach allows the auditor, on the one hand, to reliably assess the rationalization of materials supply-planning in the enterprise, and on the other hand, to recognize the degree of optimization of the procurement process in the organization's logistics system. For this purpose, it is necessary to estimate the market primary demand (independent needs) and secondary (dependent needs),[3] which will become the basis for the auditor to holistically evaluate the correctness of planning material needs in the enterprise. In addition to planning material needs, the logistics audit of procurement will focus its attention on:

- order processing processes (including complaints and returns),
- verification of the conformity of deliveries with orders,
- methods of assessment, verification, and relations with suppliers,
- degree of speed, response, and flexibility of the operation of the entire supply subsystem,
- bottlenecks in supply logistics processes,
- costs of handling orders,
- free flow of information and financial and material resources in procurement processes.

Among the areas of interest in the logistics audit of procurement presented above, special attention should be paid to the issue related to the assessment, verification, and – ultimately – selection of suppliers. The point is that the right choice of suppliers is one of the most important issues in the field of supply logistics. Therefore, the activities of the logistics audit of procurement in the sphere of supplier selection should focus primarily on (Jezierski, 2007b):

- assessment of the choice of suppliers – it is necessary to take into account which supplier best meets the requirements presented to the customer, what distance separates the supplier from the supply warehouse, what the rhythmicity and timeliness of deliveries is, what the quantitative and qualitative possibilities of deliveries in emergency situations (i.e., crisis or emergency) are,
- analysis of the form of cooperation with suppliers – the type and form of the concluded contract, provisions on the possibility and conditions of negotiating prices, rules on contractual penalties, the duration of the cooperation agreement, and the provisions on its prolongation may be verified,
- examination of elements of the supply subsystem related to the quality of supply – identifying, verifying, and improving mechanisms (persons, tools, and footnotes) supervising the quality of supply deliveries,
- review whether the supplier can be considered a so-called qualified supplier – examining the list of qualified suppliers in terms of their competence and ability to meet the criteria set for them by the recipient.[4]

In practice, the logistics audit of procurement in the sphere of suppliers should be carried out more often in relation to strategic suppliers, since it is on their supplies that the possibility of continuing the core business of the enterprise depends.

Finally, it should be emphasized that procurement logistics should be carried out especially in production enterprises, where a significant part of the costs of the production process are those resulting from procurement. In this type of organization, the purchase price of raw materials, materials, or parts strongly determines the costs of finished products, which, in the final stage, has an impact on the margin achieved from the sale of the organization's goods.

3.2. Logistics audit of production

Discussing the issues related to the logistics audit of production requires – in the first place – familiarization with the basic concepts in the field of production theory, which will determine the shape, form, and structure of this type of audit. Therefore, the terms discussed at the beginning of this chapter will refer primarily to what the product, production (production process), and production management are. So, when it comes to the definition of the word "product," it should be emphasized that often in economics it is focused strictly on the consumer, i.e., the user of a specific product or service, who always perceives the product (or service) through the prism of broadly understood applications. Meanwhile – especially in the context of participants in the production process – "product" is a term interpreted differently by the production manager, the financial manager, or the personnel manager. In the case of the former, the product will be everything that "builds" the product, i.e., production area (hall), tools, machines, processes, operations, etc. Thus, the optimal, and therefore the most beneficial in given conditions, use of the possessed set of goods will be conducive to the creation of final products that will be characterized by a high level of market competitiveness. For people dealing with enterprise finances, a product is primarily a set of different costs that shape the final price of the product and – what is important – determine its break-even point.[5] The product is perceived differently by people who deal with human resources management in the organization on a daily basis. For them, the product is the skills and qualifications of employees that are necessary to produce a specific type of product or service. To sum up, it can therefore be assumed – in a broad sense – that a product is a thing with material or immaterial characteristics, which serves to satisfy the specific needs of specific people. In practice, all products are manufactured in the production process. So far, in management science, the word "production" has received rich interpretation and many definitions. One of the most concise is that production is the activity of producing some goods and/or services. However, the production of goods, as Duda (1997) rightly points out, also requires adequate materials, a human labor force, and the necessary technical skills. In other words, production is a process – taking place in a certain time and space – that transforms available resources (material and intangible) into finished products, thus satisfying the needs of individuals, households, societies, and nations. The issue of the production process satisfying the specific needs of others was also raised in the definition presented by Hicks, in which production is any activity planned to meet the needs of others through exchange (Aliyu, 2019). Bearing in mind the definitions of production proposed by Hicks and the authors of this study, there arises the fundamental question whether the production of goods – within the framework of economics – that does not take into account the context relating to the necessity of satisfying, by these goods, the specific needs of individuals, can be considered production in the strict sense. The answer appears to be no. In economics we consider as production only those activities related to the provision of goods and services to the market that serve to meet the specific needs of consumers. This means that in economics the terms production and manufacturing should not be used interchangeably, because they are not equivalent terms. In practice, the production process can be carried out in three basic ways (Nassab et al., 2013):

- production by disintegration, which consists of separating the content of a given substance or agent from the main product. An example are the modern technologies that use a porous material called polystyrene acrylate and sunlight to separate salt from seawater. As a result of using this technique, we obtain products in the form of sea salt and drinking water,

- production by integration, which in practice is the opposite of production by disintegration and consists in combining (merging) various components into one whole. As a result, we get the product we want that satisfies our needs. An example is a building material in the form of dry concrete, which is formed by mixing cement, aggregate, additives, and a small amount of water,
- production by services, which boils down to the "refinement" of the product as a result of the activities (services) to which it is subjected. An example is the production of a diamond, which is made by grinding a diamond (precious stone) according to a diamond cut (a service performed by a jeweler).

Considering the above, we see that production is in fact a transformative activity that concerns not only goods but also services. As a result, the input data is transformed into output data, which can change in terms of form, shape, structure, volume, weight, place, or time. The end result of this process, however, is a definite good that has value, both utilitarian and economic.

The last concept, apart from product and production, which needs clarification in the context of a logistics audit of production, is production management. In a narrow sense, production management should be understood as planning, organizing, directing, and controlling processes related to the production activity of the enterprise, which are aimed at transforming – in an optimal way – raw materials into final products. However, in broad terms, production management can be defined as a holistic system of management that transforms input resources into products and services desired by consumers. Although the definitions presented above do not express it directly, it should be emphasized that the responsibility for the production process lies both with the management of the organization and with the employees who are to jointly implement specific goals according to the adopted rules, schedules, and specifications. The result of their collective work, done correctly, may be the creation of an effective production management system, which we will be able to talk about only if the goods delivered to the recipient meet quality and quantity expectations, while maintaining optimization in the implementation of production processes.

Moving directly to the issue of logistics audit of production, it should be noted at the outset that not only in management literature but also in professional and trade journals, the subject of logistics audit of production is

– to date – little discussed. This situation is caused by several factors. First of all, the logistics audit of production is a novelty on the market of audit services both in Poland and abroad. Secondly, industry audits (to which logistics audit belongs) are positions that are still poorly established in both theory and practice. Thirdly, there is a noticeable lack of specialists who could skillfully combine several years of experience in the field of logistics with their competences in the field of internal audit. And fourthly, the last gap is in the formation of professional groups or associations, which would be bodies bringing together specialists, advisors, managers, and scientists in the field of logistics and audit, whose task would focus primarily on building and developing the framework of the logistics audit methodology. Therefore, taking into account the above-mentioned limitations, which slow down the dynamics of knowledge growth in the field of the logistics audit of production, it is important to define its essence. In broad terms, a logistics audit of production is an evaluation of production logistics, which takes into account the identification of processes requiring improvement and places where unjustified production costs arise. Thus, through the logistics audit of production, one of the key principles regarding the management of the organization is implemented, related to the optimization of the costs of doing business. In a narrow sense, we will define the logistics audit of production as advisory and management activities aimed at all aspects related to the improvement of the production process, in areas related to production planning, procurement, storage, marking, reporting, and the flow of raw materials inside the production hall. Therefore, we can conclude that, in practice, a logistics audit of production is a diagnosis of the current state of production, which is the result of partial assessments, in the form of:

- an organization of work in the area of production,
- a process of planning, organizing, and controlling production,
- a flow of raw materials, semi-finished products, semi-finished products,
- a method of algorithmizing and parameterizing production,
- a system of comprehensive management of the organization through quality (total quality management (TQM)),[6]
- internal logistics (internal transport),[7]
- forces of purchasing and warehouse economies affecting the production process,
- production losses,
- a system of information flow and communication in the production process.

The main goal of the logistics audit of production is to add value and increase the degree of functionalization of the production logistics of a given enterprise, through factual and conceptual support of the decision-making process in the area of the logistics system of the organization. However, in order to achieve the basic goal, auxiliary purposes are to be used, which include:

- a thorough assessment of enterprise production logistics on the basis of the adopted criteria,
- improving operational activities,
- optimization of the use of the enterprise's production resources,
- reduction or elimination of groups of disturbances occurring in logistics processes related to procurement, production, distribution, transport, and storage,
- setting priorities for the proper implementation of the enterprise's production logistics.

The above-mentioned objectives of the logistics audit of production are implemented with the help of various methods,[8] techniques, and research tools, including document research, analysis of existing data (data mining,[9] business intelligence[10]), quantitative analyses, observations, tests, interviews, case studies, physical measurements, key performance indicators,[11] etc. Due to the fact that the logistics audit of production is a voluntary service, and therefore not resulting from the provisions of the law, it can be used by every enterprise, production- and distribution-oriented, and any others. Therefore, neither the specificity of the enterprise (its size or structure), nor the scope of its activity, nor the sector or industry in which it operates are relevant here. In other words, the recipients of the services in the form of the logistics audit of production can be all organizations whose representatives want to check and identify imperfections occurring in the production logistics system subordinate to them. The key factors determining the choice of a logistics audit of production as a tool to optimize activities in this area include:

- the need to rationalize production costs,
- the need to identify and eliminate sources affecting the inefficiency of the entire production area,
- the desire to increase labor productivity,
- the intention to improve the planning and organization of production,
- the need to reorganize and functionalize the layout of the production hall,
- the need to ensure an optimal level of stocks for critical products,
- the need to report, control, and monitor the production process,
- the desire to eliminate many disturbances occurring in the production process,

- the intention to reduce the number of complaints,
- the need to ensure traceability of serial numbers or production batches,
- the need to improve logistics parameters,
- the desire to increase the motivation and knowledge of employees about the implemented improvements.

Thus, the benefits that an organization can derive from including a logistics audit in the process of improving the efficiency of operational components of the logistics system are as significant and real as they are numerous and diverse. First, the organization's managers can count on the correctness of diagnoses made in problem areas that have been the subject of audit research. Second, taking into account the most favorable solutions in given conditions, managers can count on the fact that the decisions taken will save both time and financial resources. Third, thanks to the audit, the organization can be sure that the solutions used are a derivative of the best patterns and techniques that have been developed in this field so far. Fourth, the possibility of making incorrect decisions to protect the organization against losses related to the cost of risk are minimized. And fifth, an organization can focus on what it does best and what it specializes in.

To sum up, it should be emphasized that the logistics audit of production, when regularly conducted, builds large data sets on the logistics system of the organization, which, when properly transformed, will provide information and knowledge about the possibilities of improving its efficiency (Voortman, 2004).

3.3. The logistics audit of the warehouse

The subject of this chapter is the logistics audit of the warehouse. The discussion of this issue will be preceded by the presentation of the basic conceptual apparatus, which, on the basis of theory, is to provide a better understanding of the described category. The basic concepts permanently tied to the logistics audit of the warehouse include warehouse, warehousing, and warehouse management. On the basis of logistics, a warehouse can be concisely defined as a place of storage (keeping) of goods. However, if we wanted to refer to more extensive definitions of this concept, it is worth noting the one developed by Gołembska (2007a), in which a warehouse is a unit dealing with the storage of material products that are temporarily excluded from use, having a space separated for this purpose, as well as technical means intended for the transport of stocks and their handling. Nevertheless, the term is described by Bartholdi and Hackman (2006), for whom it is a facility in the supply chain for the consolidation of products in order to reduce transport costs and achieve economies of scale in production or purchasing. Although each of the definitions presented above emphasizes the various features of a warehouse, their common denominator is that a warehouse is an object (building) that has a specific function related to the storage of goods (materials). And although an important function, it is not the only one that warehouses perform in many organizations. A conceptual category closely coupled with warehouses is warehousing. In theory, it has received many interpretations and definitional approaches. This is a result of the different perspectives from which researchers approach this issue. Nevertheless, in a broad sense, as proposed by Razik et al. (2017), warehousing is defined as a process that groups all the activities that permit a warehouse to be designed, defines the means and tools necessary for its functioning, identifies warehouse operations, and effectively manages them. Both in theory and practice, the process related to warehousing[12] consists of four basic phases:[13] the receipt phase, the storage phase, the picking phase, and the shipment of material goods. All of them must be properly planned, organized, and controlled. However, the storage and picking phases deserve special attention, especially by managers, as they are the most complex and labor-intensive among all phases. In addition, they largely determine the level of warehouse performance. As the course of the storage process can be multidimensional and multithreaded at the same time, it is graphically presented in Figure 3.2. The last element that needs to be explained, in the context of considering the logistics audit of a warehouse, is the concept of warehouse management. The function it performs in the management of the efficient enterprise is important because it is the warehouse, as part of the logistics infrastructure, that implies the flow of resources, materials, and finished products between suppliers and final recipients. In synthetic terms, warehouse management is an activity consisting of managing the technical, organizational, and economic aspects of the warehouse's operation in the field of receiving, storing, picking, and issuing goods, while maintaining constant control over the processes and functions carried out. Thus, warehouse management focuses on the control and optimization of complex warehouse and distribution processes and is interdependent both on the tasks assigned to it and on the market in which the warehouses operate (DeKoster & Smidts, 2013). However, due to the dynamic development of the digital economy, effective warehouse management cannot be currently implemented without the participation of tools whose construction is based on artificial intelligence technology or machine-learning algorithms.

Having basic knowledge in the field of business logistics and warehousing, we can proceed to discuss the concept of the logistics audit of the warehouse. From a definitional point of view, a logistics audit of the warehouse – in synthetic terms – is an assessment of the state of warehouse logistics of an enterprise in the area of cargo planning and management

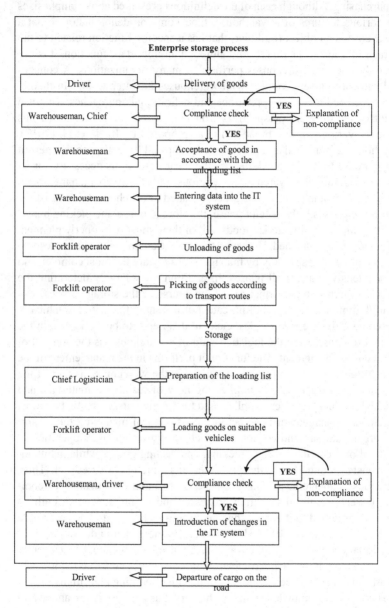

Figure 3.2 Storage process in the organization – graphical example Source: Rut and Miłasiewicz, 2016, p. 27.

and their handling in the field of receiving, storing, and shipping. Its scope covers all aspects of the enterprise's operation related to storage, including the improvement of processes and functions that are carried out in the warehouse and its close surroundings. Thanks to the evaluation – in terms of quality or complexity – of the stream of warehouse activities processing input elements into output elements, the productivity and efficiency of warehouse logistics is improved. As a consequence, activities in the entire transport and warehouse chain, which is the basis for the functioning of the supply chain in the organization, are also improved.

The logistics audit of the warehouse, like the logistics audit of production or distribution, is discretionary. This means that the management has full freedom in its planning and organization, in relation to both the organizational unit located inside the organization and to an external institution. In a narrow sense, we will understand the logistics audit of the warehouse as a thorough analysis of the elements (and the links between them) included in the storage subsystem of the enterprise's logistics system, the purpose of which is to get to know it, examine it, draw conclusions, and make the correct diagnosis in the way it operates. At the same time, this type of approach to the definition of a logistics audit of the warehouse cannot fail to take into account the impact that external factors have on warehouse processes, even in the legal and administrative dimension of the environment of each organization. The common denominator for the presented definitions is primarily the desire of the logistics audit to identify and then improve problem areas that affect the work of the warehouse, which then affects the overall logistics potential[14] of the organization. In general, a logistics audit of the warehouse has a number of goals to achieve, which can be divided into general and partial (specific). The general purposes of the logistics audit of the warehouse include:

- identification of problem areas, limitations, deviations, and inefficiencies in the sphere of warehouse management of the organization,
- optimization of warehouse logistics costs,
- increasing the degree of efficiency of activities carried out in the area of storage and warehouse management,
- reducing or eliminating errors and/or aberrations occurring in warehouse operations,
- increasing the efficiency of inventory management,
- optimization of warehouse space,
- identification and elimination of activities that do not add value to the storage subsystem of the organization's logistics system.

However, among the partial objectives of the logistics audit of the warehouse, we can distinguish:

- increasing the efficiency of processes carried out in the storage subsystem of the organization's logistics system,
- improvement of the strategy and directions of development of warehouse logistics,
- optimization of operating costs in the areas of storage, maintenance of warehouses, and utilities,
- increasing the use of people's potential and warehouse and handling infrastructure,
- elimination of bottlenecks in warehouse processes,
- increasing the productivity of the warehouse by increasing the degree of its automation,
- identification and elimination of activities that do not add value.

The implementation of selected goals that the logistics audit of the warehouse in the logistics system of the organization has to meet gives rise, in practice, to important knowledge about both the efficiency of its operation and the degree of use of its logistics potential, especially in the area of warehouse management. As a result, the management team have objective information about the state of the enterprise's logistics and can use it to correctly formulate strategies and directions for the development of warehouse logistics or to redefine them. The question arises about the additional benefits that the organization can additionally derive from the implementation of a logistics audit of the warehouse. In synthetic terms, they may concern:

- the ability to make the right decisions that save time, money, and resources of the enterprise,
- the reduction of risks, including human error risk, financial risk, operational risk, market risk, business risk, or even bankruptcy risk,
- reducing operating costs and opportunity costs,
- better use of the tangible and intangible resources of the enterprise,
- the possibility of adopting solutions that have been recognized as "best practice" in the global economy,
- the possibility of focusing on important activities and abandoning non-important ones (prioritization of tasks),
- strengthening and improving the internal control system,
- improving efforts to achieve sustainable warehouse management.

At the end of this chapter devoted to the issue of warehouse logistics audit, it should be added that this type of industry audit may cover a fragment, a part, or an area of warehouse logistics, as well as the entire spectrum of issues related to it. Thus, the research subject of logistics audit of the warehouse is the broadly understood "warehouse reality," which consists of warehouse infrastructure, handling infrastructure, warehouse IT systems, warehouse documentation, flow of materials, and information and financial resources in warehouse management. In addition, it also covers the processes, relationships, dependencies, or relationships that occur between the elements of the storage subsystem in the enterprise's logistics system. All the above-mentioned elements can be tested from the point of view of logistical audit in various aspects and using various research methods, including observational, statistical, comparative, diagnostic, heuristic,[15] documentary, or experimental research. In other words, this means that in practice, the logistics audit in warehousing is not limited, either in terms of the scope itself, the methods adopted to scientifically understand the problems of warehouse logistics, or the size of the organization that may be subject to it.

3.4. Logistics audit of distribution

Nowadays, it is impossible to imagine the functioning of an enterprise without a supply chain, which is considered one of the most extensive processes in the science of organization and management. Its holistic understanding, taking into account the product life cycle, sales service, or disposal, is often referred to as the value chain (or Porter's value chain).[16] The point is that in the process of producing goods, all the elements present in it determine the final value that the organization provides to the environment, both task-oriented and general. An inseparable part of the supply chain – in addition to supply and production – is distribution, which is considered a key element of the economic process. Due to its place in the enterprise's logistics activities, it plays a leading role in achieving its economic and marketing objectives. In practice, this is confirmed by the increase in enterprise profitability indicators,[17] which are conducive not only to its stabilization and development but above all to higher profits. This means that a well-thought-out distribution model integrated with the other subsystems of the enterprise's logistics system can become an element of fundamental importance in the winning strategy of each organization. The very concept of distribution based on management science[18] is defined as a process – i.e., a sequence of successive causally related changes – of the movement of goods between the producer and the consumer. As Domschke and Schild (1994) point out, the goods produced are prepared in a coordinated manner according to their type and size and taking into account space and time, so that delivery deadlines can be met or the volume of demand on the market can be met.

In broad terms, we can therefore conclude that distribution describes all the logistics related to the delivery of the enterprise's products and services to the recipient, taking into account their final place, delivery time, and costs. However, the proper course of this process will be the result of the degree of integration of the physical flow of goods, information, and financial resources with the functions carried out within the organization in the areas of planning, organization, and control. Nowadays, distribution, as one of the most important links in the logistics chain, is the fastest-growing sphere of logistics activity in economies, especially in developing countries. What's more, at the level of enterprises, it is often set as a benchmark in defining their market successes or failures.[19] The main goal of distribution is primarily to guarantee the fastest possible course of the process while maintaining the most favorable level of quality of consumer service in given conditions. Simply put, in other words it is about managing the supply chain in such a way that the flow of materials, information, and financial resources between the supplier and the end user will make it as fast as possible. However, in addition to the main goal, distribution also has to achieve a number of other, no less important, so-called side goals, which will include (Śliżewska & Zadrożna, 2014):

- optimization of order handling,
- optimization of the transport process,
- minimizing the time of distribution processes in such a way that the product reaches the final recipient as soon as possible,
- improving the level of consumer service,
- minimization of distribution costs,
- selection of an appropriate distribution channel.

In practice, the implementation of even a few of the selected goals referred to here can be a real challenge for the enterprise. Activities that on the one hand assume, for example, constant improvement of the level of quality of services provided among customers, and on the other hand, regular reduction of costs, are problematic in their implementation. Therefore, achieving goals in the area of distribution requires the management of the enterprise to make many decisions and perform a number of tasks; if these are not mutually exclusive, the desire to implement them in combination requires a lot of commitment and knowledge. All this must be supplemented and supported by organizational and coordination activities, because any disturbances in this respect may ultimately affect the success or failure of the organization in its pursuit of the strategic goal.[20]

The concepts inextricably linked to the distribution process, as evidenced by logistics itself, are distribution logistics and distribution channels. Distribution logistics is an activity that focuses on the implementation of activities in the sales network, from production planning to customer after-sales service. Thus, the activities carried out as part of distribution logistics cover a wide range of issues, starting from the study of market needs and the assessment of demand for the offered products, through production and sales, ending with customer service, including the after-sales service (Nowakowska, 2019). In an enterprise, distribution logistics can appear both as an element of marketing or as a normal distribution activity. In the first of these cases, distribution consists mainly in managing the activities of suppliers, production processes, optimizing the flow of products from suppliers to potential buyers to meet their requirements, while in the second, in the physical flow of products from the starting point to the destination, at the lowest possible costs and using specific distribution channels (Śliżewska & Zadrożna, 2014). Nowadays, the keen interest in distribution logistics among the managers of enterprises results from the need to gradually reduce relatively high distribution costs, especially in relation to the constantly growing competition and decreasing profitability of enterprises. In addition, alternative solutions are constantly being sought to achieve new competitive advantages of the enterprise on the market, not only in the areas of customer service standards but also – and perhaps above all – of the product. The second of the previously mentioned concepts is the distribution channel in which all distribution operations and activities are performed. The distribution channel is defined in management literature, e.g., by Oklander (2005) and Larina (2005), as a chain arranged linearly by operations, which helps the physical flow of the product from one intermediary to another, up to the end user. In other words, we can say that the distribution channel is in practice a collection of all entities through which (deliberately) there is a real flow of goods, services, information, and financial resources. At this point, it should be added that planning, and then building, a distribution channel is in practice a difficult task. Andjelkovic and Radosavljevic (2020) argue that it often poses many problems and raises the need to make important – from the point of view of the enterprise – decisions and choices regarding the type of channel (direct, indirect), number of entities involved, coverage (long, short), width (narrow or wide), and type of intermediaries (wholesaler, retailer, agent), In the context of this, Figure 3.3 shows – in simple terms – the existing possibilities for designing distribution channels, taking into account those elements referred to.

At this point it should be emphasized that the choices and the activities that the managerial staff undertakes and implements in the area of distribution channels and distribution logistics affect the holistic assessment of the degree of effectiveness of the distribution system[21] of an enterprise. As a result, the efficiency of distribution (see Figure 3.4) indicates the level of its ability to achieve the set goals, generate higher turnover from the sale of products and services, and gain a privileged position on the market in relation to other entities operating on it.

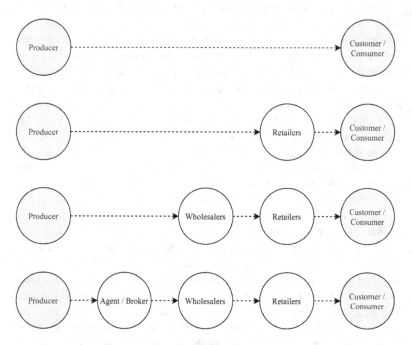

Figure 3.3 Typology of distribution channels – a comparative approach Source: Authors' own study based on Kotler (2010, p. 420).

The conceptual framework in the field of distribution logistics presented above provides a good basis for an attempt to define the logistics audit of distribution as one of the types of logistics audit. We can therefore assume that the logistics audit of distribution is – in broad terms – a systemic and expert look at the distribution subsystem in the enterprise's logistics system, in order to determine whether it meets the expectations and requirements set for it by the organization's stakeholders. However, in a narrow sense, it is an independent study consisting of acquiring (new) knowledge in the areas of storage, transport, inventory management, order fulfillment, and marketing, the aim of which is to assess the actual state of the distribution subsystem, including its potential, as well as to recommend improvement activities. In practice, the logistics audit of distribution will therefore focus on a systematic review of the entire distribution activity of the organization, in terms of the effectiveness of using its tangible and intangible resources, as well as the correctness of the functioning of processes. In addition, it will also indirectly assess the distribution potential of the organization in the logistics of the entire enterprise (see Figure 3.5).

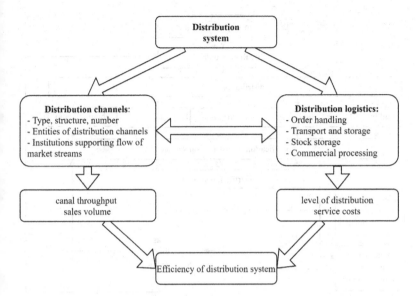

Figure 3.4 Efficient distribution system model Source: Authors' own study based on Altkorn (2004, p. 196).

Its main objectives, as an industry audit in the field of logistics, primarily include:

- assistance in making better decisions regarding the development of the enterprise's distribution system,
- assessment of whether the resources and potential of the distribution subsystem in the enterprise's logistics system are in line with the current requirements and capabilities both in terms of the whole and the components,
- identification of the strengths and weaknesses of distribution activities and systems supporting them,
- minimizing risks and accidents related to the functioning of distribution logistics,
- increasing customer satisfaction with internal and external customers from improving the quality of network operation and distribution channels,
- development of recommendations to implement the improvements proposed as a result of the logistics audit of distribution.

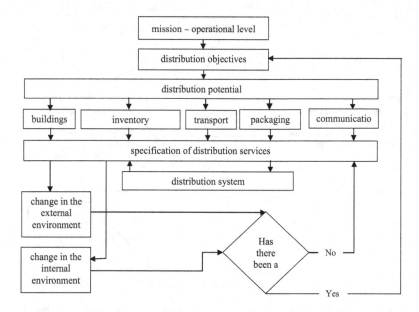

Figure 3.5 Distribution potential of the organization – reference conditions Source: based on Emerald Publishing Limited (1988, pp. 78–82).

Since the logistics audit of distribution is a complex issue, there are a large number of areas that can be subject to it in the enterprise logistics system. Nevertheless, most often, the logistics audit of distribution is subject to:

- technical and organizational distribution of the logistics network,
- structure, layout, type of flowing streams, and entities of distribution channels,
- vertical and horizontal integration of distribution channels,[22]
- processes including such activities as managing relations between entities involved in the delivery of products to end users, the flow and movement of goods, organizing and supervising the flow of information and financial resources, building sales channels, etc.,
- route of flow of materials, information, financial resources, and documents,
- ways, methods, and techniques for designing and organizing distribution,
- cost-creating areas of distribution logistics (see Table 3.1 and Figure 3.6),
- optimization of distribution transport.

Table 3.1 Logistics audit of distribution – cost-creating areas

Internal environment	Product costs	Seasonality Costs of distribution of new products
	Distribution model	Stocks Storage Use of the fleet Level of customer service Shopping
	Type of object	Procurement costs Warehouse costs Transport costs Inventory costs Overheads
External environment	Marketing factors	Transport costs Warehouse costs Inventory maintenance costs
	Competition	Location of competitors Strength of competitors
	Distribution channels	Channel structure Costs of distribution channels
	Government regulations	Manufacturers Transport Storage Packaging

Source: Authors' own study based on Lancioni, 1991, pp. 13–14.

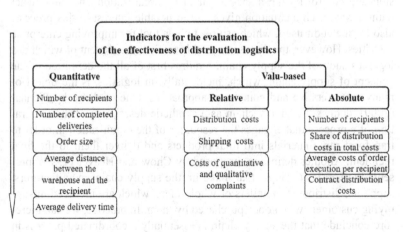

Figure 3.6 Assessment of distribution logistics Source: Authors' own study based on Nowicka-Skowron (2000, p. 29).

In the conclusion of this chapter on the issue of logistical audit of distribution, a few general remarks should be made. First, the logistics audit of distribution, as a type of logistics audit, although not yet recognized, makes an important contribution to the development of industry audits, as a modern tool supporting the basic functions carried out in the area of organization management. Second, it provides managers with valuable information on the appropriateness and effectiveness of the existing distribution subsystem in the enterprise's logistics system and the quality of its operation. Third, the distribution logistics audit provides an opportunity to identify those areas within the enterprise's distribution logistics that have the greatest capabilities and potential for "self-development." Fourth, it is a tool for critically assessing the activities of those responsible for supervising the enterprise's distribution logistics. And fifth, such audits promote pro-developmental changes in the area of broadly understood business distribution logistics and act as a catalyst for development processes in the logistics systems of the organization.

3.5. Logistics audit of the supply chain

Today, due to the global nature of most enterprises, supply chains are becoming longer and therefore more complex. As a consequence, this leads to an arithmetic increase in the risk of disruption, which in the context of the supply chain is perceived as something that requires special supervision and control by the management of an organization. In a somewhat natural way, such a situation gives rise to notable interest in this process, also for the audit itself, which aspires to be a tool for improving enterprise activities. However, the discussion in this section, the content of which is a logistics audit of the supply chain, requires first of all the definition of the concept of supply chain, which, incidentally, in logistics, is the object of many interpretative and contextual approaches. One of them, by Pienaar (2009), defines the supply chain as a synthetic description of the integration of a process that engages the resources of the organization in order to transform raw materials into final products and deliver them to the final recipient. Another definition, proposed by Chow and Heaver (1999), presents the entities (groups) that make up the supply chain: manufacturers, suppliers, distributors, retailers or wholesalers, which are involved in supplying customers with goods purchased by them. In practice, we can therefore conclude that the supply chain is essentially a coordinated process in which goods physically flow from their place of origin to their destination, accompanied in parallel by the flow of funds, intangible resources, and information (see Figure 3.7).

Knowledge of the term supply chain now entitles us to try to define the essence of the issue, which in this chapter is the logistics audit of the supply

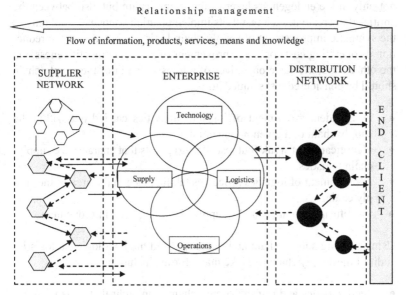

Figure 3.7 Integrated supply chain Source: based on Handfield and Nicols, 2002, p. 39.

chain. Thus, through a logistics audit of the supply chain, we understand a process aimed at improving the physical flow of goods, financial resources, intangible resources, and information in the supply chain, in order to increase its efficiency within a given organization. Improving the supply chain in the area of logistics audit consists both in the use of best practices and practices that are used in other industries and sectors and in the use of quantitative and qualitative research methods and techniques. Their final results are the basic material for developing new concepts, ideas, and solutions in modernizing the productivity of supply chains. A logistics audit of the supply chain is therefore a key tool with which management can identify and then solve the root causes of problems that occur in supply-chain logistics. Their scale, complexity, and multifaceted nature can take on different characters and be present at different levels of the organization, including at the strategic, operational, or tactical levels. What's more, gaps and deviations may also manifest themselves in the further internal environment of the enterprise, in relation to its suppliers, customers, strategic partners, co-operators, etc. A logistics audit of the supply chain is therefore a comprehensive audit that covers a wide spectrum of events that occur not only in the endogenous layer of the supply chain but also between the entities that create it. As a result, its implementation contributes not only to the synthetic improvement of supply-chain logistics, but also to the reduction of operating costs or the improvement of market competitiveness. On the other hand, the basic objectives of a logistics audit of the supply chain should be considered tasks aimed at:

- independent assessment of logistics activities carried out within the supply chain of a given organization,
- identification of weak (but also strong) points that characterize supply-chain logistics,
- improvement of logistics processes taking place in the area of the supply chain,
- identification of areas in the supply chain that need improvement.

Using existing supply-chain audit concepts and methodologies, a logistics audit of the supply chain can take many forms, including:[23]

- deep logistics audit of the supply chain – an audit that aims to familiarize itself precisely and thoroughly with the logistics processes taking place in the supply chain of an enterprise, taking into account its organizational structure, adopted business model, purchasing and supply structures, organizational environment, and competences and qualifications,
- comprehensive logistics audit of the supply chain – an audit that covers all logistics processes taking place in the subsystems of the logistics system related (directly or indirectly) to the supply chain,
- simple logistics audit of the supply chain – an audit that may concern a selected logistics process (its part or a single task) in the supply chain,
- quick logistics audit of the supply chain – an audit carried out in a short period of time, which is characterized by a narrow form, dedicated mainly to senior management, consisting in conducting simple research aimed at quickly identifying the problem and inhibiting activities that may directly affect the profit and loss account of an entity. These types of audits, however, require quick access to high-quality data.

The forms of the logistics audit of the supply chain presented above can, in practice, be carried out in various enterprises, including technological, production, trade, retail, export, import, or service. Nevertheless, in order for a logistics audit of the supply chain to be considered – apart from its form – as effective, in practice it must meet several basic conditions. First, it requires securing adequate human resources necessary to prepare an audit plan, carry out audit activities related to data collection and analysis, monitor the audit process, or develop results and proposals for improvements. Second, every audit – not only the one concerning the logistics audit of the supply chain – requires high-level specialist knowledge, which is why it should involve in its activities those people who have qualifications adequate to the subject of the tasks performed and the challenges awaiting them. Third – although it is not conclusive – the effectiveness of the audit is often determined through the prism of good knowledge of the organization, the environment in which it operates, its stakeholders, local customs, and accepted norms of behavior or values professed in an environment. Fourth, the aim should be to ensure that the audit is carried out primarily *in situ* rather than remotely, especially where there are differences of a linguistic, national, cultural, and even religious or political nature. Fifth, the measurement tools used in the audit should reflect the content, scale, and complexity of the issues examined. And sixth, an effective audit cannot do without providing adequate access to large amounts of high-quality data.

Taking into account the above, but also the contemporary conditions in which supply chains operate, it should be concluded that the implementation of a logistics audit in this area may be a difficult task, requiring also – and perhaps above all – knowledge of the concept of supply chain management. The point is that in many organizations there are different models of the supply chain, which are harmonized with the specifics of their activities. This gives rise to further challenges in the implementation of a logistics audit in this area, especially since the supply chain can be not just a single enterprise but the entire network cooperating on the basis of delivery and receipt of goods. In addition, the flows carried out in these chains may concern not only materials or finished products, but also cash, human and technological resources, and information. The latter can also come both from internal sources and from outside the entire system. What's more, the flows are "driven" by all entities that participate in the supply chain, and whose number can reach up to several units, depending on the length of the chain. The situation becomes even more complicated if it turns out – which is not difficult to imagine from the perspective of the development of modern enterprises – that we are dealing with an international supply chain. In such a case, logistics activities within the supply chain are carried out across and beyond the borders of different countries.[24] At this point, it is important to mention the numerous processes that we deal with in the supply chain, which are also in the circle of interest in auditing and concern (Douglas, 2008):

- customer relationship management,
- supplier relationship management,

- customer service management,
- demand management,
- order fulfillment,
- manufacturing flow management,
- product development and commercialization,
- returns management.

Since the above-mentioned processes are often interrelated, the auditor's identification of the root causes of problems that may arise in these areas may require constant and detailed research.

In conclusion, we can see that the supply chain is a complex and complicated issue that indirectly determines the nature of the logistics audit itself carried out in this field, thus making it difficult to implement. It is also worth noting that due to time or resource constraints, logistics audits of the supply chain usually focus their attention on one selected element, which in turn makes it difficult to obtain a holistic view of the functioning of the entire supply chain in the organization. Due to the fact that nowadays we observe an increase in the complexity of many supply chains, it is likely that we should also expect an increase in the scope and number of logistics audits carried out in this area.

3.6. Control and analytical questions

Control questions

1. Provide a definition of a logistics audit of production and specify its primary and auxiliary purposes.
2. Provide a definition of a logistics audit of a warehouse and present its general objectives.
3. Define the following concepts: distribution, distribution logistics, distribution channel, distribution logistics audit.
4. Name the quantitative and qualitative indicators for evaluating the effectiveness of distribution logistics.
5. Present procurement logistics goals by task and activity.
6. Present the definition and basic objectives of the logistics audit of procurement.
7. Provide a definition of supply chain and logistics audit of the supply chain.
8. Define and define the basic objectives of a logistics audit of the supply chain.
9. Describe the forms that a logistics audit of the supply chain can take.
10. Replace the basic processes taking place in the supply chain.

Analytical questions

1. On the basis of practice, the objectives of the logistics audit of production are implemented with the help of various methods, techniques, and research tools. With this in mind, name three of them and describe how to apply them.
2. In your opinion, how can the organization benefit from the implementation of a logistics audit of the warehouse? Justify your answer.
3. Characterize the areas, along with the type of costs that are generated in them, which may be of interest to the logistics audit of distribution.
4. Present the arguments for the fact that the logistics audit of distribution is an important tool to support the management of the organization in achieving its strategic goals.
5. Why is a logistics audit of the supply chain a type of industry audit, the implementation of which is demanding and often raises many problems? What is it caused by? Justify your answer using appropriate argumentation.

Notes

1 These include all work items that are consumed once and completely in a production cycle. According to the definition used by the Central Statistical Office, materials also include non-durable objects (tangible current assets gradually consumed in the production process), parts of machinery and equipment, useful production waste, as well as packaging.
2 Purchasing in practice boils down to the actual (physical) act of buying goods (service).
3 Independent needs (primary demand) are needs resulting from customer demand for the final goods of the enterprise. It is a demand strongly determined by the market, which is why it is always characterized by a certain level of unpredictability (uncertainty). As for dependent needs (secondary demand), they result from primary demand, the structural structure of the product, as well as the technology used and the organization of production. In practice, this is the demand for materials and other elements needed to produce final products. Importantly, with a specific structure of demand, the demand is determined based on direct calculations and is therefore not subject to any degree of uncertainty.
4 The verification procedure of qualified suppliers implemented in an enterprise should also be analyzed.
5 Product profitability is the ability of a product to generate profit from every dollar obtained from the market. In other words, we consider a profitable product to be a product whose sales revenues exceed its overall costs (including production, marketing, promotion, etc.).
6 TQM is a management technique based on the assumption that all employees of the organization constantly improve their skills and improve their competences in order to achieve maximum customer satisfaction with the products and/or services it offers.

7 It includes the internal movement of raw materials, components and sub-assemblies from warehouse halls, storage points and side production lines to the so-called production cells. Internal logistics also includes transport and picking of ready-to-load products and transport.

8 Quantitative, qualitative, and those bearing the characteristics of a scientific experiment.

9 A process of analyzing large data sets in terms of looking for anomalies, deviations, paradigms, or correlations in order to predict final results based on them.

10 Business analytics, which in practice is an action of transforming data into useful information and knowledge.

11 Key performance indicators (KPIs) are measures by which management can constantly monitor the progress of the organization in achieving the assumed goals, including the implementation of the strategic goal.

12 Krzyżaniak et al. (2014) define the storage process as "operations relating to the temporary receipt, storage, completion, movement, maintenance, recording, inspection and delivery of goods."

13 In the receipt phase, the delivered goods are unloaded and identified, and are then sorted. At the same time, they are inspected both quantitatively and qualitatively. In practice, the acceptance phase is the stage of preparing the goods for their storage. The second phase – storage – involves the receipt of goods from the reception zone and placing them in the storage zone (i.e., the arrangement of the assortment in the warehouse zone). In this zone, the goods are periodically inspected and then issued to the picking area. During the picking phase, stock sets are created according to quantitative and assortment specifications for the defined customer. In other words, at this stage, it is about the preparation of a completed order for the recipient/customer. The final stage of the storage process is the release phase. In this part of the process, the packaged items are formed into transport units and then sent from the warehouse to the specified customers.

14 In the opinion of Brzeziński (2005), logistic potential is a function of logistic capabilities, which are dynamic and time-varying quantities. Thus, their evaluation can only be carried out within a defined time frame under precisely defined conditions that take into account the restrictions existing for a given period of time. The cardinal elements of the logistics potential defined in this way include human potential, material potential, technical potential, and management potential.

15 The essence of heuristic methods, which do not belong to the methods of creation but rather are conducive to creation, is to arrive at original and innovative solutions through discovering new facts, contacts, and relationships taking place in reality. More information on this subject can be found in Martyniuk's book *Introduction to Invention*, second edition, which in 1997 was published by the University Publishing House of the Cracow Academy of Economics (now the Cracow University of Economics).

16 The concept of the value chain was created and popularized by M.E. Porter of Harvard Business School. For more on this topic, see Porter, M.E. (1998). *Competitive Advantage: Creating and Sustaining Superior Performance (With a New Introduction)*, The Free Press, New York.

17 Also called profitability or rate-of-return indicators. They are often used in the evaluation of enterprises. However, their usefulness is largely limited by the fact that they have a high level of generality, which reduces their economic content.

18 From the Latin, *distributio*, meaning division, separation.
19 Peter Thiel, co-founder and investor of the American enterprise PayPal Holdings, Inc., and Elon Musk's business partner, in one of the interviews stated that poor distribution – not the product – is the main cause of an enterprise's market failures.
20 In the opinion of Śliżewska and Zadrożna (2014), the primary task of distribution is to fill the gaps that arise between the sphere of production and consumption, and which concern the time gap, the spatial gap, the quantitative gap, the gap in the assortment, and the information gap.
21 For more on this subject, see Frankowska, M., Jedliński, M. (2011). *Efficiency of the Distribution System*, PWE, 1st ed., Warsaw.
22 Vertical integration of distribution channels consists of linking channel entities located at different levels of distribution by means of contracts, agreements, or economic subordination. Horizontal integration, on the other hand, is a combination of the resources of two or more intermediaries within the same level of distribution who have different competences, when those intermediaries want to use them together on the basis of cooperation and mutual exchange.
23 For more on this topic, see: *Supply Chain Audit Case Study*, http://hafezicapital.com/supply-chain-audit/, [Accessed 14.01.2021].
24 See Gołembska, E. (2007b). *Basic Problems of Global Logistics, International logistics, Eurologistics*, Wydawnictwo Naukowe Wyższej Szkoły Kupieckiej, Łódź.

4 Logistics audit

A management approach

4.1. Audit – a tool for improving the organization

As Trenkner (2016) rightly points out, the need for improvement, or, precisely speaking, the need to induce the need for improvement, has been
known about for decades. Nowadays, it takes on a special meaning, especially in relation to organizations that need to prepare for digital transformation. Its scale of influence on the current manner of functioning of the
world and enterprises is best evidenced by the fact that often in the subject
literature, the noun "transformation" is replaced by the term "revolution."
Thus, we can risk the thesis that we are currently dealing with a revolution
rather than a digital transformation. This distinction seems to be important
because in the case of revolution – and unlike transformation – the changes
taking place are decisive and rapid rather than transformative. Considering
this, and the issues presented further in this chapter, it is therefore necessary
to ask ourselves a basic question about the semantic character of the terms
"improvement" or "improving." To improve means to take conscious action
in order to make something better than before. And so we can improve
not only spoken or written language or craftsmanship, but also methods,
techniques, structures, systems, or processes. Improving the latter of these
elements seems to be particularly close to any modern organization that sys-
tematically strives to be more efficient, more effective, or more flexible and
thus quickly adapt to the changing environment around them. In general,
we can even conclude that an organization's pursuit of excellence[1] (being a
role model for others in the market), in all its possible areas and aspects, has
become in recent years an *idée fixe* for a significant number of managers.
Indirectly, Kozina (2014) also draws attention to this, arguing that the conditions in which modern organizations operate, including a turbulent environment, global dimension of competitiveness, and rapid development of
technology, somehow force them to constantly improve management tools
in various areas of the company's activity. In this regard, let us note that not

DOI: 10.4324/9781003380184-5

assets and liabilities, is transferred to another entity. Although the two terms are often used interchangeably, they describe two distinct situations: A merger is the consolidation of two companies to create a new legal entity under the banner of one corporate name, whereas an acquisition occurs when one company takes ownership of another (Cartwright and Schoenberg, 2006). Although M&As can be complicated due to the large number of investors involved in crowdfunding, they represent, together with IPOs, a valuable exit choice for companies that use this type of investment. Signori and Vismara (2018), for example, find evidence that among equity crowdfunded firms in their sample, 1.4% were involved in M&A deals with positive returns. Cumming *et al.* (2019b) investigate the impact of the ownership structure of companies that have successfully completed an equity crowdfunding campaign on the British platform Crowdcube on their ability to deliver an exit opportunity through an M&A or an IPO. The authors find evidence that interest alignment between ownership and control improves the likelihood of exit through an IPO or an M&A.

4.3.3 *Initial public offerings*

One of the possible (albeit rare) post-campaign scenarios for crowdfunded companies is represented by the initial public offerings (IPOs). An IPO refers to the process of offering shares of a private company to the public in a new stock issuance for the first time. This process allows companies to 'go public', that is, to transition from private to public ownership. The literature on IPOs identifies several motivations for why companies choose to go public (see Celikyurt *et al.*, 2010, among others). Companies typically pursue an IPO to raise additional capital that can be used to expand the business, fund research and development, or pay off debt. Other important motivations for going public include: funding growth initiatives, strengthening the company's public profile, giving founders the ability to diversify their risk, letting insiders cash out, or allowing venture capitalists and early investors in the company to exit their investments by selling some or all of their private shares as part of the IPO. Finally, some scholars suggest that the desire to be acquired may be a primary driver of the IPO decision and that entrepreneurs can undertake an IPO to prepare their company for sale as part of a larger M&A process (Reuer and Shen, 2003). On the sell side, searching for potential acquirers is costly, as well as time-consuming and extremely resource-intensive. On the buy side, small private companies are generally difficult to locate as exchange partners and have more difficulty signalling their business prospects to investors. As a consequence, assessing their value can pose significant difficulties for buyers who often tend to prefer public targets over private targets when acquiring smaller and younger businesses (Shen and Reuer, 2005). The literature on IPOs has shown that the move from the private to the public domain facilitates the sale of the company by increasing its visibility and disclosure and reducing the asymmetric information faced by potential acquirers. In addition, a post-IPO acquisition allows the target company to obtain a higher valuation and, therefore, be acquired at a more attractive price than a direct acquisition as a private company (Shen and Reuer, 2005). Consistent with the above arguments, some scholars have confirmed that smaller and younger companies have a higher likelihood of becoming takeover targets after their IPOs (Gao *et al.*, 2013).

Given the insufficient liquidity of secondary markets for equity crowdfunding (Lukkarinen and Schwienbacher, 2023), IPOs can represent an important exit route for crowd investors, allowing them to fully realise the gains from their investment (Signori and Vismara, 2018). However, IPOs are rare events for crowdfunded companies as they are usually too small and cannot afford the high initial compliance costs of a typical IPO (which include extensive due diligence, hiring a legal counsel and an underwriter, Securities and Exchange Commission – SEC – registration fees, market listing fees, and more) (Cumming *et al.*, 2019b). Although the percentage of companies that get through this exit is extremely low, some equity-crowdfunded companies have turned out to be extremely successful in undergoing IPOs (Blaseg *et al.*, 2020).

4.3.4   Firm failure

Beyond the potential benefits of crowdfunding that could attract future equity investors, there are some costs (e.g., equity dilution, communication costs with large pools of investors, among others) that could cause drawbacks in the long run, including firms' failure.

Walthoff-Borm *et al.* (2018) investigate the post-campaign financial and innovative performance of 205 firms financed with equity crowdfunding between 2012 and 2015 on the UK platforms Crowdcube or Seedrs. Matching equity-crowdfunded firms (ECF) and non-equity-crowdfunded (NECF) firms, the authors find empirical evidence that ECF firms have 3.4 times higher patent applications and 8.5 times higher failure rates than matched NECF firms. The authors also find that direct and nominee shareholder structures are associated with firm performance; indeed, ECF firms financed through a nominee structure make smaller losses, whereas ECF firms financed through a direct shareholder structure have more new patent applications. Signori and Vismara (2018) found a low failure rate among equity crowdfunded firms; only 17.9% of the firms in their sample failed after successfully raising funds through equity crowdfunding, and none of these failed firms had previously been supported by qualified investors. Hornuf *et al.* (2018)

analyse failure rates and follow-up funding of 413 equity crowdfunded firms in Germany and the United Kingdom between 2011 and 2016. The empirical evidence shows that German crowdfunded firms are more likely to attract follow-up funding from venture capitalists or business angels but, at the same time, they are also more likely to fail than British firms. According to the authors, follow-up funding is positively influenced by the number of senior managers and initial venture capital investors and is negatively influenced by the average age of the senior management team. Firms failure is positively impacted by the number of initial venture capital investors and the firm's valuation and is negatively impacted by the number of senior managers and the amount raised during previous equity crowdfunding campaigns. In a recent study, Blaseg *et al.* (2020) provide evidence that firms that are tied to riskier banks and use equity crowdfunding are more likely to fail compared to those that are more experienced and financially successful. The authors attribute these results to the fact that equity crowdfunding can attract low-quality firms, with lower liquidity buffers and greater leverage, which rely on the inexperience of crowd investors to obtain financing.

References

Atherton, A. (2012). Cases of start-up financing: An analysis of new venture capitalisation structures and patterns. *International Journal of Entrepreneurial Behavior & Research*, 18(1), 28–47. 10.1108/13552551211201367.

Beck, T., & Demirguc-Kunt, A. (2006). Small and medium-size enterprises: Access to finance as a growth constraint. *Journal of Banking & Finance*, 30(11), 2931–2943. 10.1016/j.jbankfin.2006.05.009.

Behr, P., Entzian, A., & Güttler, A. (2011). How do lending relationships affect access to credit and loan conditions in microlending?. *Journal of Banking & Finance*, 35(8), 2169–2178. 10.1016/j.jbankfin.2011.01.005.

Berger, A. N., & Udell, G. F. (1995). Relationship lending and lines of credit in small firm finance. *Journal of Business*, 68(3), 351–381.

Blaseg, D., Cumming, D. J., & Koetter, M. (2020). Equity crowdfunding: High-quality or low-quality entrepreneurs? *Entrepreneurship Theory and Practice*. 10.1177/1042258719899427.

Block, J. H., Colombo, M. G., Cumming, D. J., & Vismara, S. (2018). New players in entrepreneurial finance and why they are there. *Small Business Economics*, 50, 239–250. 10.1007/s11187-016-9826-6.

Brown, R., Mawson, S., Rowe, A., & Mason, C. (2018). Working the crowd: Improvisational entrepreneurship and equity crowdfunding in nascent entrepreneurial ventures. *International Small Business Journal*, 36(2), 169–193. 10.1177/0266242617729743.

Bruton, G., Khavul, S., Siegel, D., & Wright, M. (2015). New financial alternatives in seeding entrepreneurship: Microfinance, crowdfunding, and peer-to-peer innovations. *Entrepreneurship Theory and Practice*, 39(1), 9–26. 10.1111/etap.12143.

Carpenter, R. E., & Petersen, B. C. (2002). Is the growth of small firms constrained by internal finance?. *Review of Economics and Statistics*, 84(2), 298–309. 10.1162/003465302317411541.

Cartwright, S., & Schoenberg, R. (2006). Thirty years of mergers and acquisitions research: Recent advances and future opportunities. *British Journal of Management*, 17(S1), S1–S5. 10.1111/j.1467-8551.2006.00475.x.

Celikyurt, U., Sevilir, M., & Shivdasani, A. (2010). Going public to acquire? The acquisition motive in IPOs. *Journal of Financial Economics*, 96(3), 345–363. 10.1016/j.jfineco.2010.03.003.

Coakley, J., Lazos, A., & Liñares-Zegarra, J. M. (2022). Seasoned equity crowdfunding offerings. *Journal of Corporate Finance*, 77, 101880. 10.1016/j.jcorpfin.2020.101880.

Cole, R. A., Goldberg, L. G., & White, L. J. (2004). Cookie cutter vs. character: The micro structure of small business lending by large and small banks. *Journal of Financial and Quantitative Analysis*, 39(2), 227–251. 10.1017/S0022109000003057.

Colombo, M. G., & Shafi, K. (2021). Receiving external equity following successfully crowdfunded technological projects: An informational mechanism. *Small Business Economics*, 56(4), 1507–1529. 10.1007/s11187-019-00259-1.

Cumming, D. J., Johan, S. A., & Zhang, Y. (2019a). The role of due diligence in crowdfunding platforms. *Journal of Banking & Finance*, 108, 105661. 10.1016/j.jbankfin.2019.105661.

Cumming, D. J., Meoli, M., & Vismara, S. (2019b). Investors' choices between cash and voting rights: Evidence from dual-class equity crowdfunding. *Research Policy*, 48(8), 103740. 10.1016/j.respol.2019.01.014.

Cummings, M. E., Rawhouser, H., Vismara, S., & Hamilton, E. L. (2020). An equity crowdfunding research agenda: Evidence from stakeholder participation in the rulemaking process. *Small Business Economics*, 54, 907–932. 10.1007/s11187-018-00134-5.

Da Cruz, J. V. (2018). Beyond financing: Crowdfunding as an informational mechanism. *Journal of Business Venturing*, 33(3), 371–393. 10.1016/j.jbusvent.2018.02.001.

Diamond, D. W. (1991). Monitoring and reputation: The choice between bank loans and directly placed debt. *Journal of Political Economy*, 99(4), 689–721. 10.1086/261775.

Drover, W., Busenitz, L., Matusik, S., Townsend, D., Anglin, A., & Dushnitsky, G. (2017a). A review and road map of entrepreneurial equity financing research: Venture capital, corporate venture capital, angel investment, crowdfunding, and accelerators. *Journal of Management*, 43(6), 1820–1853. 10.1177/0149206317690584.

Drover, W., Wood, M. S., & Zacharakis, A. (2017b). Attributes of angel and crowdfunded investments as determinants of VC screening decisions. *Entrepreneurship Theory and Practice*, 41(3), 323–347. 10.1111/etap.1220.

Eldridge, D., Nisar, T. M., and Torchia, M. (2019). What impact does equity crowdfunding have on SME innovation and growth? An empirical study. *Small Business Economics*, 1–16. 10.1007/s11187-019-00210-4.

Estrin, S., Gozman, D., & Khavul, S. (2018). The evolution and adoption of equity crowdfunding: Entrepreneur and investor entry into a new market. *Small Business Economics*, 51, 425–439. 10.1007/s11187-018-0009-5.

Ferri, G., & Murro, P. (2015). Do firm–bank 'odd couples' exacerbate credit rationing?. *Journal of Financial Intermediation*, 24(2), 231–251. 10.1016/j.jfi. 2014.09.002.

Gao, X., Ritter, J. R., & Zhu, Z. (2013). Where have all the IPOs gone?. *Journal of Financial and Quantitative Analysis*, 48(6), 1663–1692. 10.1017/S0022109014 000015

Giudici, G., Guerini, M., & Rossi-Lamastra, C. (2020). Elective affinities: Exploring the matching between entrepreneurs and investors in equity crowdfunding. *Baltic Journal of Management*, 15(2), 183–198. 10.1108/BJM-08-2019-0287.

Hall, B. H. (2010). The financing of innovative firms. *Review of Economics and Institutions*, 1(1), 1–30. 10.5202/rei.v1i1.4.

Hall, B., & Lerner, J. (2010). The financing of R&D and innovation. In B. H., Hall and N. Rosenberg (eds.), *Handbook of the Economics of Innovation* (pp. 609–639). North-Holland: Elsevier. 10.1016/S0169-7218(10)01014-2.

Hernández-Cánovas, G., & Martínez-Solano, P. (2010). Relationship lending and SME financing in the continental European bank-based system. *Small Business Economics*, 34, 465–482. 10.1007/s11187-008-9129-7.

Hornuf, L., Schmitt, M., and Stenzhorn, E. (2018). Equity crowdfunding in Germany and the United Kingdom: Follow-up funding and firm failure. *Corporate Governance: An International Review*, 26(5), 331–354. 10.1111/corg.12260.

Hyytinen, A., & Pajarinen, M. (2008). Opacity of young businesses: Evidence from rating disagreements. *Journal of Banking & Finance*, 32(7), 1234–1241. 10.1016/j.jbankfin.2007.10.006.

Kaminski, J., Hopp, C., & Tykvová, T. (2019). New technology assessment in entrepreneurial financing–Does crowdfunding predict venture capital investments?. *Technological Forecasting and Social Change*, 139, 287–302. 10.1016/j.techfore.2018.11.015.

Kirschenmann, K. (2016). Credit rationing in small firm-bank relationships. *Journal of Financial Intermediation*, 26, 68–99. 10.1016/j.jfi.2015.11.001.

Lopez-Gracia, J., & Sogorb-Mira, F. (2008). Testing trade-off and pecking order theories financing SMEs. *Small Business Economics*, 31(2), 117–136. 10.1007/s11187-007-9088-4.

Lukkarinen, A., & Schwienbacher, A. (2023). Secondary market listings in equity crowdfunding: The missing link?. *Research Policy*, 52(1), 104648. 10.1016/j.respol.2022.104648.

Miglo, A. (2022). Crowdfunding and bank financing: Substitutes or complements? *Small Business Economics*, 59(3), 1115–1142. 10.1007/s11187-021-00571-9.

Mochkabadi, K., & Volkmann, C. K. (2020). Equity crowdfunding: A systematic review of the literature. *Small Business Economics*, 54(1), 75–118. 10.1007/s111 87-018-0081-x.

Moro, A., & Fink, M. (2013). Loan managers' trust and credit access for SMEs. *Journal of banking & Finance*, 37(3), 927–936. 10.1016/j.jbankfin.2012.10.023.

Myers, S. C., & Majluf, N. S. (1984). Corporate financing and investment decisions when firms have information that investors do not have. *Journal of Financial Economics*, 13(2), 187–221. 10.1016/0304-405X(84)90023-0.

Petersen, M. A., & Rajan, R. G. (1994). The benefits of lending relationships: Evidence from small business data. *The Journal of Finance*, 49(1), 3–37. 10.1111/j.1540-6261.1994.tb04418.x.

Reuer, J., & Shen, J. C. (2003). The extended merger and acquisition process: Understanding the role of IPOs in corporate strategy. *European Management Journal*, 21(2), 192–198. 10.1016/S0263-2373(03)00014-8.

Ross, S. A. (1977). The determination of financial structure: The incentive-signalling approach. *The Bell Journal of Economics*, 8(1), 23–40. 10.2307/3003485.

Rossi, A., & Vismara, S. (2018). What do crowdfunding platforms do? A comparison between investment-based platforms in Europe. *Eurasian Business Review*, 8, 93–118. 10.1007/s40821-017-0092-6.

Ryu, S., Kim, K., & Hahn, J. (2019). The effect of crowdfunding success on subsequent financing outcomes of start-ups. In *Academy of Management Proceedings* (Vol. 2019, No. 1, p. 17486). Briarcliff Manor, NY 10510: Academy of Management. 10.5465/AMBPP.2019.17486abstract.

Schwienbacher, A. (2013). The entrepreneur's investor choice: The impact on later-stage firm development. *Journal of Business Venturing*, 28(4), 528–545. 10.1016/j.jbusvent.2012.09.002.

Serrasqueiro, Z. S., Armada, M. R., & Nunes, P. M. (2011). Pecking order theory versus trade-off theory: Are service SMEs' capital structure decisions different?. *Service Business*, 5(4), 381–409. 10.1007/s11168-011-0119-5.

Shen, J. C., & Reuer, J. J. (2005). Adverse selection in acquisitions of small manufacturing firms: A comparison of private and public targets. *Small Business Economics*, 24, 393–407. 10.1007/s11187-005-5332-y.

Signori, A., & Vismara, S. (2018). Does success bring success? The post-offering lives of equity-crowdfunded firms. *Journal of Corporate Finance*, 50, 575–591. 10.1016/j.jcorpfin.2017.10.018.

Stevenson, R., McMahon, S. R., Letwin, C., & Ciuchta, M. P. (2022). Entrepreneur fund-seeking: Toward a theory of funding fit in the era of equity crowdfunding. *Small Business Economics*, 58(4), 2061–2086. 10.1007/s11187-021-00499-0.

Su, L., Cheng, X., Hua, Y., & Zhang, W. (2021). What leads to value co-creation in reward-based crowdfunding? A person-environment fit perspective. *Transportation Research Part E: Logistics and Transportation Review*, 149, 102297. 10.1016/j.tre.2021.102297.

Tomczak, A., & Brem, A. (2013). A conceptualized investment model of crowdfunding. *Venture Capital*, 15(4), 335–359. 10.1080/13691066.2013.847614.

Uchida, H., Udell, G. F., & Yamori, N. (2012). Loan officers and relationship lending to SMEs. *Journal of Financial Intermediation*, 21(1), 97–122. 10.1016/j.jfi.2011.06.002.

Vismara, S. (2016). Equity retention and social network theory in equity crowdfunding. *Small Business Economics*, 46, 579–590. 10.1007/s11187-016-9710-4.

Walthoff-Borm, X., Schwienbacher, A., & Vanacker, T. (2018). Equity crowdfunding: First resort or last resort?. *Journal of Business Venturing*, 33(4), 513–533. 10.1016/j.jbusvent.2018.04.001.

Walthoff-Borm, X., Vanacker, T., & Collewaert, V. (2018). Equity crowdfunding, shareholder structures, and firm performance. *Corporate Governance: An International Review*, 26(5), 314–330. 10.1111/corg.12259.

Zheng, H., Xu, B., Zhang, M., & Wang, T. (2018). Sponsor's cocreation and psychological ownership in reward-based crowdfunding. *Information Systems Journal*, 28(6), 1213–1238. 10.1111/isj.12190.

5 The crowdfunding revolution

Looking at positive benefits from alternative finance across different dimensions

5.1 Introduction

The 2007–2008 Global Financial Crisis and the recent COVID-19 pandemic have shaken global financial markets and caused immense turmoil with unprecedented effects that will reverberate for years (Cicchiello 2022). At the same time, financial crises and economic downturns have allowed new funding channels like crowdfunding to flourish. From the birth of the first platforms to today, crowdfunding has undergone a tremendous evolution, demonstrating its ability to promote female empowerment and gender equality, support sectors, categories, and communities in difficulty (e.g., agriculture, education, green energy, culture, and more), and foster the expansion of emerging-economy financial markets. In a post-COVID world, statistics indicate that the use of crowdfunding in all its forms will continue to grow. In fact, according to a recent study conducted by Grand View Research,[1] the global crowdfunding market is projected to grow at a compound annual growth rate (CARG) of 16.7% from 2023 to 2030, resulting in a market volume of US$5.53 billion and $300 billions of total revenues by 2030.

The growth of the global crowdfunding market will be driven by the rising adoption of social media platforms such as Facebook, Twitter, Instagram, and LinkedIn for crowdfunding activities, as well as the use of technological innovations. Artificial intelligence (AI) tools, Blockchain, and machine learning technologies will allow crowdfunding platforms to further streamline the fundraising process and reduce information asymmetries and verification costs. In this way, platforms will be able to better select companies and detect fraud and other deceptive behaviour by companies, mitigating investors' concerns about the truthfulness of the information provided. All these factors are expected to create profitable growth opportunities for the crowdfunding market players in the coming years.

DOI: 10.4324/9781003381518-6

5.2 Crowdfunding for cultural and creative industries

The concept of cultural and creative industry (CCI) has evolved over time, gradually including an increasing number of activities and adapting to technological advances and the rapid social, economic, and cultural changes that have taken place in society.

To this day, there is still no universally accepted definition of the term 'cultural and creative industry' (Galloway and Dunlop, 2007). Differences in definitions adopted at the national level largely depend on the multidimensional and multi-faceted nature of cultural and creative activities and on the presence of different approaches in local public policies aimed at supporting this industry.

According to the European Commission (2018, page 21), the CCIs refer to all activities aimed at the development, the creation, the production, the distribution, and the preservation of goods and services based on cultural values or artistic and other collective or individual creative expressions. The CCIs comprise the following fields and sectors: architecture, archives, libraries and museums, artistic crafts, audio-visual (including film, television, video games, and multimedia), tangible and intangible cultural heritage, design, festivals, music, literature, performing arts, books and publishing, radio, and visual arts.

The CCIs are mainly populated by micro, small, and medium-sized enterprises, non-profit organisations, individual companies, and freelancers for whom the fulfilment of cultural and creative ideas and the expression of their own artistic skills are generally more important than achieving financial objectives (i.e., increase profits and sales) (Chaston, 2008). Most cultural and creative entrepreneurs regard themselves as 'creative practitioners' with a peculiar entrepreneurial identity that mixes together aspects of both traditional entrepreneurship and cultural and creative principles (Werthes *et al.*, 2018).

The CCIs have a strong impact on the development and the competitiveness of the European economy, especially for countries with a rich cultural heritage such as those in the Mediterranean region that often lag behind the core European countries (Rubio Arostegui and Rius-Ulldemolins, 2020). According to the official data from the Eurostat Structural Business Statistics (SBS), in 2019 the CCIs accounted for about 4.4% of the total EU GDP in terms of turnover (approximately €643 billions of annual revenues). The CCIs represented also a leading sector for job creation, with around 1.2 million businesses employing more than 7.3 million workers in the EU-27 (approximately 3.6% of the total EU workforce). Figure 5.1 shows the number of enterprises active in the cultural sectors in 2019 per country. Figure 5.2 shows the cultural employment (i.e., all persons employed having either a cultural profession or working in the cultural sector) according to the

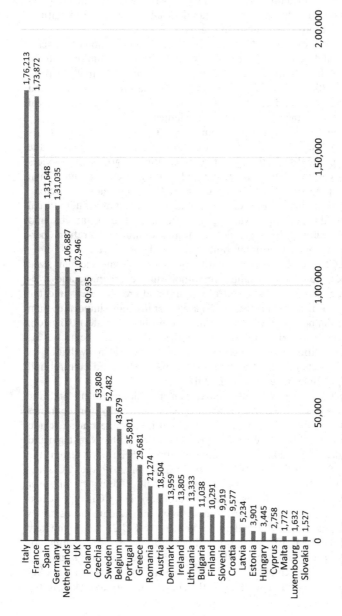

Figure 5.1 Number of enterprises in the cultural sectors per country in 2019.

Source: Author's elaboration on data from Eurostat, the statistical office of the European Union.

Note: For some countries (such as Czechia, Luxembourg, and the United Kingdom) data for 2019 were unavailable. In this case, data from the latest available year (i.e., 2018) was used in order to provide statistics for as many countries as possible.

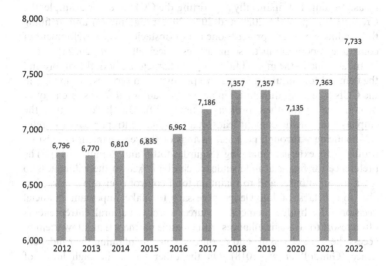

Figure 5.2 Cultural employment by NACE Rev. 2 activity EU-27, 2012–2022 (1,000 persons).

Source: Author's elaboration on data from Eurostat, the statistical office of the European Union.

Note: For the United Kingdom, data up to 2019 have been included. Data for Cyprus refer only to the areas of Cyprus controlled by the Government of the Republic of Cyprus. Since 2014, data for France include also the French overseas departments (Guadeloupe, Martinique, Guyane, and La Réunion), with the exception of Mayotte.

NACE (Nomenclature générale des Activités économiques dans les Communautés Européennes) Rev.2 statistical classification of economic activities in the EU-27 from 2012 to 2022.

In a global context, CCIs play a crucial role in attracting foreign investment, encouraging the export of cultural goods and services, strengthening Europe's global attractiveness, and promoting European cultural identity on the world stage (European Commission, 2018). In addition to their economic contribution, CCIs support health, social cohesion, and well-being, promote ethics and education in the moral values, and enhance inclusion at the individual, community, and societal levels (Pratt and Jeffcutt, 2009; OECD, 2021). It is therefore not surprising that since the mid-1980s CCIs have entered the political agendas of all governments around Europe which have sought to unlock their full potential from an economic and social perspective (Rubio Arostegui and Rius-Ulldemolins 2020). Both national and European cultural policies provide for the implementation of numerous public measures aimed at financially supporting the CCIs (see, for example, the Creative Europe 2014–2020 and 2021–2027 programmes) and at filling the funding gap that represents one major obstacle to the development of companies operating in these industries (Cicchiello *et al.*, 2022a).

In fact, due to the market failures that characterise both the supply and the demand for cultural and creative products and services, companies in the CCIs face great difficulties in accessing traditional forms of equity or debt financing for their projects (Frey, 2019). On the one hand, the emphasis on artistic content leads many cultural entrepreneurs to prefer self-financing – through personal savings or the reinvestment of existing profits – to external financing (Sigurdardottir and Candi, 2019). The preference for financial independence can be linked to the willingness to work autonomously and to maintain total control over one's work, but also to the lack of knowledge necessary to make important financial decisions. To bridge financial resource scarcity, cultural entrepreneurs often resort to strategic alliances with creative partners that allow them to access the necessary skills and resources while maintaining their independence (Gundolf *et al.*, 2018). On the other hand, the high levels of uncertainty and unpredictability in consumers' reaction to new cultural and creative products increase the risk of product failure making it difficult for creative entrepreneurs to attract investments (Caves, 2000). Funding challenges in the CCIs also depend on the difficulties that banks and other financial institutions encounter in attributing the right value to the intangible assets on which cultural and creative activities are strongly based (Borin and Donato, 2015).

Consequently, companies in the CCIs have been (and still are today) mainly financed – directly or indirectly – by public funds through the provision of grants and subsidies or tax relief (OECD, 2022).

Cutbacks in public and private funding for the CCIs – exacerbated first by the 2007–2008 Global Financial Crisis and recently by the COVID-19 crisis – have highlighted the need for a more diversified financial ecosystem for cultural and creative companies combining public, private, and alternative sources of financing that can meet their various financing needs (De Propris, 2013; Khlystova *et al.*, 2022).

Over the last few years, crowdfunding has established itself as a main subset of the alternative financial sources available for the CCIs (Cicchiello *et al.*, 2022b). Crowdfunding for the CCIs (also known as 'cultural and creative crowdfunding') offers companies and professionals in the sector the opportunity to finance their works by circumventing the judgement of a small group of experts (whose decision-making processes are often opaque and characterised by gender discrimination and favouritism) and directly addressing the diversified audience of internet users, without geographical or network constraints (Mollick and Nanda, 2016). Crowdfunding provides financial support for the implementation of cultural and creative products and services despite the contrary opinion of experts, especially in sectors like gaming or music where crowd investors represent the final consumers of the products and services in question.

Although the availability of recent data on crowdfunding in CCIs is limited, the study by De Voldere and Zeqo (2017) carried out for the European Commission reveals that from 2013 to 2016 around 247 million euros were raised by companies in the CCIs through over 75,000 crowdfunding campaigns. Also, according to the study, 88% of the campaigns took place on a reward-based crowdfunding platform, the model mainly used by cultural entrepreneurs, artists, and businesses in the CCIs. Crowdfunding platforms are established throughout Europe, with a higher concentration in Italy, France, Germany, and the United Kingdom.

Table 5.1 shows the number of crowdfunding platforms operating in the CCIs displayed for each type of crowdfunding model, including donation-based crowdfunding, reward-based crowdfunding, and investment-based crowdfunding (i.e., equity and lending models). Hybrid platforms are those that combine two different crowdfunding models (e.g., donation and reward). The number of crowdfunding platforms is divided into 'cultural and creative platforms' (i.e., platforms exclusively dedicated to cultural and creative projects) and 'general platforms' (i.e., platforms dedicated to at least one category of the CCIs). Up to November 2022, out of 78 platforms, 51 are dedicated to rewards; 18 of these are pure cultural crowdfunding platforms. Donation-based and investment-based are less used models (eight and six total platforms, respectively).

Table 5.2 shows the complete list of platforms referred to in Table 5.1 by foundation year, country, model, and sector focus (cultural and creative vs. general).

Table 5.1 Number of crowdfunding platforms operating in the CCIs by type of crowdfunding model

	Number of platforms		
	General	*Cultural and creative*	*Total*
Donation	5	3	8
Reward	33	18	51
Investment	2	4	6
Hybrid	11	2	13
Total	51	27	78

Source: Author's elaboration on data from crowdfunding4culture.eu.

Table 5.2 List of crowdfunding platforms by foundation year, country, model, and sector focus

Platform	Foundation year	Country	Model	Sector focus
100-days.net	2012	Switzerland	Donation and Reward	General
100Fans	2013	Germany	Reward	Cultural and Creative
4just1	2010	Netherlands	Donation	General
52 Masterworks	2014	Germany	Investment	Cultural and Creative
Addact	2013	Germany	Reward	Cultural and Creative
Adjukössze	1994	Hungary	Donation	General
Adrifund	2016	Slovenia	Donation and Reward	Cultural and Creative
Adrifund	2016	Slovenia	Reward	Cultural and Creative
Art Fund	2012	Slovenia	Donation	Cultural and Creative
Bandbackers	2014	the United Kingdom	Investment	Cultural and Creative
BeCrowdy	2013	Italy	Reward	Cultural and Creative
Bidra	2014	Norway	Reward	General
Boekensteun	2013	Belgium	Donation	General
Boekensteun	2013	Belgium	Donation	Cultural and Creative
BookaBook	2011	Italy	Reward	General
Bookabook	2014	Italy	Reward	Cultural and Creative
Booomerang.dk	2011	Denmark	Reward	General
Buona Causa	2010	Italy	Donation and Reward	General
CineCrowd	2011	Netherland	Reward	General
CineDime	2014	Germany	Investment	Cultural and Creative
CoopFunding	2016	Spain	Donation and Reward	General
Corrective	2002	Germany	Donation	Cultural and Creative
Crowd Thinking	2012	Spain	Reward	General
Crowd'in	2014	Belgium	Reward	General
Crowdbooks	2011	Italy	Reward	General
Crowdfunder	2010	the United Kingdom	Reward	General

CrowdFundMe	2010	the United Kingdom	Donation	General
CrowdPatch	2016	the United Kingdom	Reward	General
Culture Time	2014	France	Donation and Reward	General
Dartagnans	2014	France	Reward	Cultural and Creative
Derev	2013	Italy	Donation and Reward	General
DigVentures	2012	the United Kingdom	Reward	Cultural and Creative
Eppela	2011	Italy	Reward	General
Fund it	2011	Ireland	Reward	Cultural and Creative
Fundsurfer	2014	the United Kingdom	Reward	General
Ginger	2013	Italy	Reward	General
Global Rockstar	2014	Austria	Donation and Reward	General
Goteo	2012	Spain	Reward	General
Growfunding	2013	Belgium	Reward	Cultural and Creative
HitHit	2012	Slovakia	Reward	Cultural and Creative
Hooandja	2011	Estonia	Reward	Cultural and Creative
Karolina Fund	2012	Iceland	Reward	Cultural and Creative
Kiss Kiss Bank	2013	France	Reward	General
Lanzanos	2011	Spain	Reward	General
Libros	2011	Spain	Reward	General
Megatotal	2007	Poland	Reward	Cultural and Creative
Mesenaatti.me	2012	Finland	Reward	General
Multifinantare	2012	Romania	Investment	Cultural and Creative
Musicstarter	2014	Germany	Reward	General
My Major Company	2007	France	Reward	Cultural and Creative
Nordstarter	2010	Germany	Reward	General
Polak Potrafi	2013	Poland	Reward	General
PPL	2011	Portugal	Reward	General
Proarti	2009	France	Donation and Reward	General
Produzioni dal Basso	2005	Italy	Donation and Reward	General

(Continued)

Table 5.2 (Continued)

Platform	Foundation year	Country	Model	Sector focus
Projektu Banka	2015	Latvia	Reward	General
Raizers	2014	France	Investment	General
Show4Me	2014	the United Kingdom	Reward	Cultural and Creative
Socrowd	2005	the United Kingdom	Investment	General
Spacehive	2011	the United Kingdom	Donation	General
Spieleschmiede	2015	Germany	Reward	General
Startlab	2017	Slovakia	Reward	Cultural and Creative
Startovac	2013	Czech Republic	Reward	General
Tilburgvoorcultuur	2013	Netherland	Reward	Cultural and Creative
Totsuma	2013	Spain	Donation and Reward	General
Touscoprod	2009	France	Reward	General
Ulule	2010	France	Reward	General
Unbound	2011	the United Kingdom	Reward	General
Verkami	2010	Spain	Reward	General
VersPers Crowdpress	2014	Netherland	Donation and Reward	General
Vision Bakery	2010	Germany	Reward	General
VoordeKunst	2011	Netherland	Reward	General
Wemakeit	2011	Switzerland	Reward	General
World of Mass Development	2015	the United Kingdom	Reward and Investment	Cultural and Creative
Wspieram	2010	Poland	Reward	General
Wspieramkulture	2012	Poland	Reward	Cultural and Creative
Youcan2	2012	Spain	All	General
Zaar	2015	Malta	Reward	General

Source: Author's elaboration on data from crowdfunding4culture.eu.

Data from Tables 5.1 and 5.2 have been hand collected from the website 'Crowdfunding4Culture' (www.crowdfunding4culture.eu), a European-wide information hub about crowdfunding in the cultural and creative sectors founded in February 2016. The website includes a map of all crowdfunding platforms in Europe in the CCIs from which the names of 158 platforms were extracted. Only native platforms (i.e., those with headquarters in Europe) were considered, while foreign platforms operating in Europe but based in other countries, such as the US platforms Indiegogo and Kickstarter, were excluded. After manually checking the websites of each of the listed platforms, another 80 platforms were excluded either because they lack a functioning website and therefore considered no longer active, or because they lack active cultural and creative projects. This leads to a total number of 78 native platforms operating in Europe in the cultural and creative sector.

The emergence of crowdfunding as a valid alternative tool for the financing of companies in CCIs has increasingly attracted the attention of researchers who have mainly focused on three research areas: (i) the success determinants of crowdfunding projects, (ii) the motivations for using crowdfunding, and (iii) the non-financial benefits of crowdfunding for companies in the CCIs (Cicchiello *et al.*, 2022a).

The literature on success determinants of crowdfunding projects is certainly the broadest line of research, not only for the specific case of the CCIs but for crowdfunding in general. The majority of empirical studies in this field analyse data from Kickstarter, one of the largest platforms for projects in the CCIs with nearly half of hosted campaigns that successfully meet their funding goals. Mollick (2014) was perhaps the first to use Kickstarter's extensive data to analyse the dynamics behind campaign success and failure. The author identifies several key signals of the projects' quality that can increase their chances of being successfully funded, such as the inclusion of a project presentation video, the provision of frequent updates immediately after the project is launched, and an account on a social network (Facebook in this case) with a large number of connections. Finally, the author investigates the role of geography in the campaigns' success by finding evidence of a positive connection between the proportion of creative individuals in the founder's city and the chances of having a successful campaign. With a focus on successful and failed filmmaking campaigns launched on Kickstarter between December 2012 and February 2013, Hobbs *et al.* (2016) uncover key drivers of crowdfunding success. These include: (i) campaign characteristics (i.e., the number of rewards offered in exchange for the contribution received, the number of updates about the project, the campaign length, and the number of supporters); (ii) social network characteristics (i.e., the number of Facebook friends and shares, the number of Facebook and Twitter connections, and the number of

Google searches related to the campaign); (iii) financial aspects (i.e., the desired target amount, the collected final amount, and the number of investors); and (iv) campaign's quality (i.e., reward- and- pitch quality). Using data from Kickstarter projects, Barbi and Bigelli (2017) reveal that the success of the campaigns is positively influenced by the presence of a presentation video, a greater number of rewards, a shorter campaign duration, and a smaller size of the funding goal. Similarly, Koch and Siering (2019) question the factors (and their interactions) that lead to the success of crowdfunding campaigns on the Kickstarter platform. The authors identify the following three factors: (i) conditions of pledging (i.e., the amount of money requested and the duration of the campaign); (ii) characteristics of the project (i.e., information disclosure through texts, videos and images, risk disclosure, and emotional appeal in the project description); and (iii) characteristics of the founders (i.e., their experience in previous crowdfunding campaigns and their popularity on social networks). Bao and Huang (2017) investigate how the three dimensions of external supports (i.e., reward, impression, and relationship) influence the performance of cultural and creative projects listed on Kickstarter in film and video and publishing categories. Regarding reward support, the study shows that ego-boosting rewards, customise rewards, and reward that fosters feelings of community belongings positively affect both the performance of projects in the film and video category and those in editorial. Results for impression support reveal that updates and comments are effective for both categories of projects, while visual elements (i.e., pictures and videos) are only effective for projects in the film and video category but not editorial ones. Finally, for relationship support, the findings show that the number of entrepreneur's Facebook friends and the 'obligations' to support other campaigns are important for crowdfunding performance of projects in both categories. Based on a sample of cultural projects launched on the Netherlands' Voordekunst platform, Borst *et al.* (2018) examine how the strength of the social media used by the creators of the projects is able to attract funding from latent ties (i.e., unknown people) as well as from strong and weak ties (i.e., friends or existing relations) and contribute positively to campaigns' success. The results show that latent ties (i.e., unknown funders) contribute more to the success of campaigns than strong and weak ties (family and friends' network). In a recent study, Tosatto *et al.* (2022) use data from the UK's PledgeMusic platform – specialised in music projects – to analyse the relationship between online communication channels used by musicians and bends to communicate with their fan communities and the likelihood of campaigns being successful. According to the authors' findings, thanks to its strong social ties, email represents a more effective online communication channel than Facebook and Twitter in converting fans into funders.

Another important stream of literature investigates the motivations for the use of crowdfunding in CCIs, both by cultural companies and entrepreneurs, and by supporters. By interviewing potential investors of the music-focus platform SellaBand, Ordanini *et al.* (2011) reveal that the main motivation behind consumers' decision-making is the opportunity to make the record of professional albums possible through their financial support. Jian and Shin (2015) investigate the contributors' dynamics in crowdfunded journalism by using data from the donation-based platform Spot.Us. Relying on the theory of collective action, the authors show that belief in freedom of content, altruism, and contribution to their communities are among the strongest motivators for donors of small contributions. On the contrary, fun and the willingness of entrepreneurs' family and friends to help them are among the main motivations for donors of largest monetary contributions who, however, contribute only once and do not return to donate a second time. These findings lead the authors to question the feasibility of crowdfunding as a sustainable business model for regular news production, especially in the donation-based form. Offering rewards to donors or allowing them to share in the profits of purchased news articles could incentivize them to participate more actively in campaigns. Bürger and Kleinert (2021) address the motivational differences between commercial backers, who support commercial entrepreneurs, and cultural backers, that support cultural entrepreneurs. The idea behind their study is that, since cultural entrepreneurs are characterised by a unique entrepreneurial profile that combines the creation of economic value with that of cultural value, they address an audience of culturally oriented supporters who appreciate art and cultural products in general and understand the needs of cultural entrepreneurs. The results show that neither of the two backers' communities is motivated by altruism and the willingness to help others selflessly; however, commercial backers seem to be more motivated by pecuniary rewards than cultural backers who are instead more motivated by community rewards.

Recently, the literature has started to analyse the non-financial benefits of crowdfunding for companies in the CCIs. Indeed, crowdfunding benefits go well beyond fundraising and can be more significant for the CCIs than other sectors due to their unique nature. Crowdfunding plays an important role in the innovation and value-creation processes by promoting knowledge transfer and knowledge spill overs. Crowdfunding facilitates interaction and active communication between creative entrepreneurs and the crowd of supporters (the potential end users), allowing the latter to offer, both during and after the campaign, direct feedback on the products that will subsequently be placed on the market. This feedback may include new ideas on ways to enhance the product and its value to consumers, leading to true collaboration in product development in the spirit of crowdsourcing. The feedback provided by the crowd can also take the form of valuable insights into the product's success beyond the crowdfunding campaign, enabling entrepreneurs to assess its future demand (Hervé and Schwienbacher, 2018). Recent empirical studies have confirmed the positive effects of crowdfunding in specific fields of the CCIs. By investigating the effects of crowdfunding in the digital game industry, Nucciarelli *et al.* (2017) find that crowdfunding allows game developers to open up their business models to end users not only to finance their projects, but above all to validate their ideas, and refine and pre-test games using user's feedback and ideas. As a consequence, users become active stakeholders in the value creation process changing the entire industry value chain. Tyni (2020) confirms the role of crowdfunding as an effective new channel for the development and production of independent games. The author also points out how the introduction of crowdfunding has resulted in the reorganisation of the game industry's production network with the roles previously associated with the publisher being redistributed among game developers (who have assumed an increasingly 'publisherly' role), supporters/future consumers, and the crowdfunding platforms (who have assumed the role of central brokers setting the terms and conditions). In contrast, Galuszka and Brzozowska (2017) show that the above positive externalities do not apply to the music market, where the democratising effect of crowdfunding is constrained by the power, connections, and know-how of traditional record labels. Based on data from the board game industry, Wachs and Vedres (2021) investigate the capacity of crowdfunding to foster innovation through the feedback provided by supporters. According to the authors, games financed through crowdfunding have distinctive and novel characteristics compared to traditionally financed ones. In particular, crowdfunded games present new and more complex combinations of the gameplay mechanisms they incorporate (i.e., the functional aspects that drive the game such as the roll-and-move mechanism: you roll the dice and then move to the next space). Furthermore, the authors demonstrate that the innovative potential of crowdfunding extends beyond individual products to the entire board game industry. The open and public nature of crowdfunding allows new game ideas – created through end-user contributions, potential customer interactions, and competitor observations – to spill over to traditionally funded games thanks to the process of imitation learning. In the light of the above, crowdfunding is seen as a disruptive innovation to the board game industry.

While not without limitations, the above studies collectively explain the importance that crowdfunding has assumed over the last few years for CCIs companies; importance that was confirmed during the serious crisis that hit the CCIs following the COVID-19 pandemic. The COVID-19 outbreak and subsequent social distancing measures have led to a shift of the CCIs towards the digital environment, creating new opportunities for the use of crowdfunding.

5.3 The role of crowdfunding in the transition towards a circular economy

The concept of circular economy (hereinafter, CE) has its roots in the need to address the serious social, economic, and environmental consequences of the fast depletion of natural resources to protect the integrity of natural ecosystems on which the survival of humanity depends. The traditional model of the linear economy predicts that raw materials are extracted to be transformed into products, which are sold, consumed, and subsequently disposed of as waste once they reach the end of their useful life.

In this type of economic system, guided by the 'take, make and dispose' philosophy, value is created by producing and selling as many products as possible without taking into account the fact that most of these products are not literally 'consumed' but become waste residues that cause serious environmental damage in terms of pollution and of squandering of water, energy, labour, and capital resources used for their production. According to the report from the environmental non-profit organisation Feedback EU (2022), the EU wastes more food than it imports (153.5 million tonnes of food wasted each year against the 138 million tonnes of agricultural products imported), causing at least 6% of the total greenhouse gas emissions and costing businesses and households more than €143 billion a year. From these alarming data emerges the urgency of a paradigm shift towards an economic system in which the ecological, economic, and social impact of production and consumption is not only minimised but even becomes positive. The main idea of the CE is based on the 3Rs principles: reduce, reuse, and recycle (Ghisellini *et al.*, 2016). The CE aims at the implementation of circular systems and new business models that eliminate waste of all kinds by the following three actions: (i) minimising the use of natural resources in the manufacturing process; (ii) reusing materials to make entirely different products; and (iii) recycling products when they no longer serve their functions to transform them into completely new products (see Figure 5.3).

In this context, production and consumption models are implemented following reparative and regenerative logics that close the energy and material cycles, preventing the depletion of natural resources and facilitating sustainable development (Geissdoerfer *et al.*, 2017). Renewable energy, collected from sources or processes that are not subject to depletion as they are naturally and constantly replenished at a higher rate than they

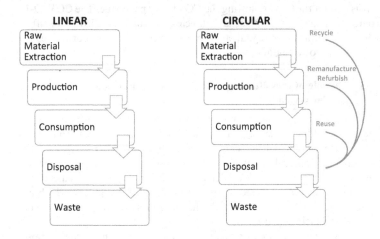

Figure 5.3 Linear economy model versus CE model.

Source: Author's elaboration.

are consumed (e.g., solar energy, wind energy, hydropower energy from flowing water, biomass energy from plants, and geothermal energy from heat inside the earth), represents the main energy source for the CE.

The CE requires companies to implement virtuous business models based on a more resource-efficient and cost-effective approach that ensures a reduction or a complete elimination of the need for virgin materials and an increase in the use of renewable energy resources to create circular products that are going to be used throughout their life. Beyond savings on manufacturing material costs, the adoption of circular business models would help companies mitigate demand-driven price volatility on raw material markets, cope with the growing pressure to address sustainability concerns, and reduce their dependence on fossil fuels (also known as 'dirty fuels'), thus protecting them from the constant fluctuations in global energy supplies and prices (Ellen MacArthur Foundation, 2015).

Given its positive potential, the transition towards a CE has acquired a priority place on the agendas of European policy makers, resulting in the adoption in 2015 of the first Circular Economy Action Plan (CEAP) and in 2020 of the new Circular Economy Action Plan (European Commission, 2020). This ambitious Action Plan, put forward by the European Commission as one of the main building blocks of the European Green Deal, aims to maximise the positive externalities deriving from the transition from a linear to a CE, minimising the costs for people and businesses. The opportunity of a CE has also gained enormous traction among academics, becoming the focus of a growing body of theoretical and empirical research (e.g., Lieder and Rashid, 2016). Recent studies revealed that, despite evidence of both short- and long-term benefits related to the adoption of more circular business models at the company level, the lack of financial resources pose formidable challenges to European companies, especially to SMEs and start-ups that usually face higher financial constraints relative to large firms (García-Quevedo *et al.*, 2020, among others). Indeed, with the exception of new companies already born according to the CE paradigm, the implementation of circular business models requires a considerable amount of time, human resources, and investments. Since in most cases SMEs and start-ups do not have the internal financial resources necessary to undertake CE activities, they have to turn to external sources of financing whose availability is however often limited due to their high-risk profile. Traditional bank financing, for example, is hampered on the supply side by banks' difficulty in assessing the risks associated with CE projects which, although not completely new, lack sufficient historical data and benchmarking. On the demand side, the lack of sufficient collateral for the loan is often the reason why businesses may be credit-constrained or excluded. Equity finance through venture capitalists and business angels represents a viable source of external financing for the transition of SMEs to a CE. However, only a small percentage of SMEs presents the profile required by private equity investors. Finally, European public funds and national government grants often do not bear the expected results, proving to be inadequate to lead an effective CE transition.

In this context, new alternative funding mechanisms such as crowd-funding can play a central role in facilitating and accelerating the transition of companies towards a CE (European Commission, 2020; Pizzi *et al.*, 2021). Crowdfunding platforms offer users the opportunity to invest in CE-oriented projects (e.g., renewable energy, clean technology, sustainable food, recycling, and so on), closing the funding gaps for new business models and, thus, contributing to the transition towards a CE (Cicchiello *et al.*, 2023).

Although the literature on the subject is still in its early phase, a growing number of studies have demonstrated the key role crowd-funding plays in moving towards a sustainable society (e.g., Testa *et al.*, 2019). Lam and Law (2016), for example, provide evidence on the importance of crowdfunding for the financing of renewable and sustainable energy projects, especially in the early stages of their life cycle. According to the authors, crowdfunding can fill the financial gap and add legitimacy to sustainable and renewable energy projects, while providing a number of advantages over traditional financial institutions in terms of: (i) lower fixed and transaction costs due to the absence of physical infrastructure, (ii) greater independence of entrepreneurs in the development of renewable projects, and (iii) greater opportunities for further venture capital investments following the crowdfunding campaign thanks to its signal effect. Vasileiadou *et al.* (2016) investigate crowdfunding for renewable electricity projects in the Netherlands with the aim of assessing its potential to finance the energy transitions towards renewable sources. The authors reveal that crowdfunding has the potential to close the funding gap for energy transition by tapping into users' financial resources. Furthermore, it can increase the societal and political support for renewable energy through the active involvement of users in renewable energy projects on crowdfunding platforms. According to Abu-Ghunmi *et al.* (2016), crowdfunding can be used as effective funding mechanisms to attract private investments of equity or debt type in the wastewater treatment industry. In a recent study, Bertoldi *et al.* (2021) count crowdfunding among the innovative financing schemes able to accelerate investments for the energy renovation of residential buildings in Europe.

5.4   Crowdfunding and female entrepreneurs' empowerment

While the European business landscape, including the start-up world, has traditionally been male-oriented, the progress made in recent times encourages hopes for a fundamental change in this trend.

Over the last few years, the European Commission has adopted a set of measures to eliminate persisting gender inequalities and reach the objectives of the EU Gender Equality Strategy 2020–2025, the Gender Action Plan 2 (GAP II) of the Horizon Europe Framework Programme for Research and Innovation 2021–2027 and, more in general, the United Nation Sustainable Development Goal (SDG) number 5: Achieve gender equality and empower all women and girls by 2030.

According to the gender statistics database of the European Institute for Gender Equality (EIGE), in 2022 men accounted for 91.4% (563) of the presidents and 97.7% (561) of the chief executive officers (CEOs) of the largest nationally registered companies listed on national stock exchanges. While women accounted only for 8.6% (53) and 8.3% (51), respectively. Although the employment rate of European women has increased to reach 54.4% in 2021 against 64.8% of men, only 9.3% of women are self-employed (i.e., are the sole or joint owner of the unincorporated enterprise in which they work) of which 2.4% with employees (i.e., employers) and 6.8% without employees (i.e., own-account workers). According to the last Women's Entrepreneurship Report published by the Global Entrepreneurship Monitor (2022), Europe shows the highest rates of gender parity in entrepreneurship compared to other parts of the world. However, the total early-stage entrepreneurial activity (TEA) rates tend to be quite low in almost all

European countries, especially in Norway, which is the country with the lowest gender ratio (1.7% women vs. 4.4% men). Spain is the only country in which the start-up activity rates for women exceed those for men (5.6% women vs. 5.4% men), while in Romania the rates are almost equal (9.6% women vs. 9.8% men). The same applies for the Established Business Ownership (EBO) rates which remain dominated by men in almost all European countries. The COVID-19 pandemic has exacerbated these gender disparities as the closure of schools and childcare centres due to lockdowns and restrictions have increased the difficulty for women entrepreneurs to combine family and work. Despite the difficulties, 12.6% of female entrepreneurs with established businesses in Europe have adopted new digital technologies in response to the pandemic, showing the existence of gender equality. Unfortunately, the rate of digitalisation was significantly lower for women entrepreneurs in the early stage of entrepreneurial activity.

These data clearly indicate that the European entrepreneurial landscape is changing to become a more inclusive arena, with women now having more opportunity to unlock their entrepreneurial and leadership potential. However, despite the progress women have made, the journey towards change is long and hard, and there is still a lot of work to be done to ensure gender equality in entrepreneurship. A great step forward in gender parity has been done with the new EU law on gender balance in corporate boards, adopted on November 2022, according to which by 30 June 2026 women in European's largest listed companies must represent at least 40% of the non-executive directors or 33% of all directors.[2]

Entrepreneurial finance literature has widely recognised the fact that women suffer gender-specific disadvantages in accessing finance, especially in the initial start-up phase. Female-led startups, for example, are much less likely than their male counterparts to receive external equity funding from venture capital firms and business angels (Poczter and Shapsis, 2018; Balachandra, 2020). At least some of this gap in funding reflects the existence of investors' prejudices and stereotypes based on gender, defined as shared beliefs about what attributes and behaviours characterise each sex[3] (Laguía *et al.*, 2019). In society, women are generally associated with the traditional familial roles of care and assistance, while leadership positions and entrepreneurial activities are seen predominantly as a male prerogative. These stereotypes about the role of women in society produces the so-called 'glass ceiling' effect: a barrier of prejudice and discrimination that leads to the common misconception that women entrepreneurs lack the knowledge and skills needed to start or run a successful business, especially in male-dominated industries. It is therefore not surprising that only a very small proportion of women-led firms raise financing from venture capitalists or angel investors who, moreover, are mostly men. Other possible reasons for differences in the funding of female-owned firms can be found in the fact that women are more risk-averse and less self-confident than men. This imbalance can in part explain the lower propensity of female entrepreneurs to ask for external financing and to prefer, instead, to satisfy their financial resource needs through informal sources that involving the assumption of lower risks such as the use of their personal savings or loans from friends and family (Coleman and Robb, 2009).

Unlike traditional financing markets that focus on companies' profitability, size, and growth, in alternative financing markets such as crowdfunding, trustworthiness may be perceived by investors as the most important aspect (Johnson *et al.*, 2018). Crowdfunding settings, especially those based on equity, are typically characterised by a severe information asymmetry between entrepreneurs and investors and great uncertainty about investment outcomes due to light regulation, the lack of institutional mechanisms and formal due diligence processes, and the fact that crowdfunded projects' initiators are generally first-time entrepreneurs with little or no track record. In these contexts, trustworthiness judgements can play a crucial role in investment decision-making, reducing perceptions of uncertainty and creating in investors a desire to 'assist' the entrepreneur considered as trustworthy (Johnson *et al.*, 2018).

According to the stereotype content theory, women by their very nature tend to be viewed as more trustworthy, generous, and upstanding than men (Fiske *et al.*, 2018). Therefore, investors who engage in crowdfunding may prefer to give their financial support to female entrepreneurs rather than male entrepreneurs (Johnson *et al.*, 2018). At the same time, investors may perceive men entrepreneurs who turn to crowdfunding as less competent than those who use traditional sources of financing such as venture capital or angel investment. Moreover, crowd investors may be more willing to support female entrepreneurs than male entrepreneurs just to promote gender equality, regardless of the actual returns on their investments. The warm glow argument (Andreoni, 1990) states that people experience a sense of joy and satisfaction (a 'warm glow' precisely) when they help others by giving time or money to good causes. Considering the altruistic nature of crowdfunding, investors may feel their investment may be more beneficial for a woman and, therefore, may feel better about financing a female entrepreneur over a male entrepreneur (Allison *et al.*, 2015).

A growing body of literature has recognised that equity crowdfunding has the power to democratise access to finance for female entrepreneurs, reducing gender inequality and giving women an edge over men (Cumming *et al.*, 2021) both in developed and developing countries (Cicchiello *et al.*, 2020; 2021). According to these studies, female entrepreneurs are more likely to succeed in equity crowdfunding campaigns than male entrepreneurs (e.g., Cicchiello and Kazemikhasragh, 2022).

By providing women with an advantage in accessing funds, equity crowdfunding stimulates the development of female entrepreneurship which represents a fundamental part of any economy, capable of generating significant contributions to economic growth, job creation, and poverty reduction (Global Entrepreneurship Monitor, 2022). Female empowerment in entrepreneurship and any other aspect of life is essential for our societies to thrive and ensure collective well-being.

Notes

1 The report is available at: https://www.grandviewresearch.com/industry-analysis/crowdfunding-market-report.
2 See https://ec.europa.eu/info/files/directive-gender-balance-corporate-boards_en.
3 See the stereotype content theory (Powell *et al.*, 2002).

References

Abu-Ghunmi, D., Abu-Ghunmi, L., Kayal, B., & Bino, A. (2016). Circular economy and the opportunity cost of not 'closing the loop' of water industry: The case of Jordan. *Journal of cleaner production*, 131, 228–236. 10.1016/j.jclepro.2016.05.043.

Allison, T. H., Davis, B. C., Short, J. C., & Webb, J. W. (2015). Crowdfunding in a prosocial microlending environment: Examining the role of intrinsic versus extrinsic cues. *Entrepreneurship Theory and Practice*, 39(1), 53–73. 10.1111/etap.12108.

Andreoni, J. (1990). Impure altruism and donations to public goods: A theory of warm-glow giving. *The Economic Journal*, 100(401), 464–477. 10.2307/2234133.

Balachandra, L. (2020). How gender biases drive venture capital decision-making: Exploring the gender funding gap. *Gender in Management: An International Journal*, 35(3), 261–273. 10.1108/GM-11-2019-0222.

Bao, Z., & Huang, T. (2017). External supports in reward-based crowdfunding campaigns: A comparative study focused on cultural and creative projects. *Online Information Review*, 41(5), 626–642. 10.1108/OIR-10-2016-0292.

Barbi, M., & Bigelli, M. (2017). Crowdfunding practices in and outside the US. *Research in International Business and Finance*, 42, 208–223. 10.1016/j.ribaf.2017.05.013.

Bertoldi, P., Economidou, M., Palermo, V., Boza-Kiss, B., & Todeschi, V. (2021). How to finance energy renovation of residential buildings: Review of current and emerging financing instruments in the EU. *Wiley Interdisciplinary Reviews: Energy and Environment*, 10(1), e384. 10.1002/wene.384.

Borin, E., & Donato, F. (2015). Unlocking the potential of IC in Italian cultural ecosystems. *Journal of Intellectual Capital*, 16(2), 285–304. 10.1108/JIC-12-2014-0131.

Borst, I., Moser, C., & Ferguson, J. (2018). From friendfunding to crowdfunding: Relevance of relationships, social media, and platform activities to crowdfunding performance. *New media & Society*, 20(4), 1396–1414. 10.1177/1461444817694591.

Bürger, T., & Kleinert, S. (2021). Crowdfunding cultural and commercial entrepreneurs: An empirical study on motivation in distinct backer communities. *Small Business Economics*, 57(2), 667–683. 10.1007/s11187-020-00419-8.

Caves, R. E. (2000). *Creative industries: Contracts between art and commerce*. Cambridge, MA: Harvard University Press.

Chaston, I. (2008). Small creative industry firms: A development dilemma?. *Management Decision*, 46(6), 819–831. 10.1108/00251740810882617.

Cicchiello, A. F., Gallo, S., & Monferrà, S. (2022a). Financing the cultural and creative industries through crowdfunding: The role of national cultural dimensions and policies. *Journal of Cultural Economics*, 1–43. 10.1007/s1 0824-022-09452-9.

Cicchiello, A. F., Gallo, S., & Monferrà, S. (2022b). Mapping crowdfunding in cultural and creative industries: A conceptual and empirical overview. *European Management Review*, 19(1), 22–37. 10.1111/emre.12510.

Cicchiello, A. F., Cotugno, M., Perdichizzi, S., & Torluccio, G. (2022c). Do capital buffers matter? Evidence from the stocks and flows of nonperforming loans. *International Review of Financial Analysis*, 84, 102369. 10.1016/j.irfa.2022. 102369.

Cicchiello, A. F., Gatto, A., & Salerno, D. (2023). At the nexus of circular economy, equity crowdfunding and renewable energy sources: Are enterprises from green countries more performant?. *Journal of Cleaner Production*, 136932. 10.1016/j.jclepro.2023.136932.

Cicchiello, A. F., & Kazemikhasragh, A. (2022). Tackling gender bias in equity crowdfunding: An exploratory study of investment behaviour of Latin American investors. *European Business Review*, 34 (3), 370–395. 10.1108/ EBR-08-2021-0187.

Cicchiello, A. F., Kazemikhasragh, A., & Monferrà, S. (2020). Gender differences in new venture financing: Evidence from equity crowdfunding in Latin America. *International Journal of Emerging Markets*, 17(5), 1175–1197. 10.11 08/IJOEM-03-2020-0302.

Cicchiello, A. F., Kazemikhasragh, A., & Monferra, S. (2021). In women, we trust! Exploring the sea change in investors' perceptions in equity crowdfunding. *Gender in Management: An International Journal*, 36(8), 930–951. 10.1108/GM-10-2020-0309.

Coleman, S., & Robb, A. (2009). A comparison of new firm financing by gender: Evidence from the Kauffman Firm Survey data. *Small Business Economics*, 33(4), 397–411. 10.1007/s11187-009-9205-7.

Cumming, D., Meoli, M., & Vismara, S. (2021). Does equity crowdfunding democratize entrepreneurial finance? *Small Business Economics*, 56(2), 533–552. 10.1007/s11187-019-00188-z.

De Propris, L. (2013). How are creative industries weathering the crisis?. *Cambridge Journal of Regions, Economy and Society*, 6(1), 23–35. 10.1093/ cjres/rss025.

De Voldere, I., & Zeqo, K. (2017). Crowdfunding: Reshaping the crowd's engagement in culture. *Publications Office of the European Union*. Available at: https://op.europa.eu/en/publication-detail/-/publication/7e10916d-677c-11e7-b2f2-01aa75ed71a1/language-en/format-PDF/source-search   (Retrieved on 14 November 2022).

Ellen MacArthur Foundation. (2015). Towards a circular economy: Business rationale for an accelerated transition. Available at: https://ellenmacarthurfoundation.org/towards-a-circular-economy-business-rationale-for-an-accelerated-transition (Retrieved on 21 November 2022).

European Commission. (2018). Proposal for a regulation of the European Parliament and of the Council establishing the Creative Europe Programme (2021 to 2027) and repealing Regulation (EU) No 1295/2013.

European Commission. (2020). A new Circular Economy Action Plan For a cleaner and more competitive Europe. Available at: https://eur-lex.europa.eu/resource.html?uri=cellar:9903b325-6388-11ea-b735-01aa75ed71a1.0017.02/DOC_1&format=PDF (Retrieved on 22 November 2022).

Feedback EU. (2022). *No time to waste: Why the EU needs to adopt ambitious legally binding food waste reduction targets.* Rijswijk, the Netherlands: Feedback EU. Available at: https://feedbackglobal.org/wp-content/uploads/2022/09/Feedback-EU-2022-No-Time-To-Waste-report.pdf (Retrieved on 18 November 2022).

Fiske, S. T., Cuddy, A. J., Glick, P., & Xu, J. (2002). A model of (often mixed) stereotype content: Competence and warmth respectively follow from perceived status and competition. *Journal of Personality and Social Psychology,* 82(6), 878–902. DOI: 10.1037//0022-3514.82.6.878.

Frey, B. S. (2019). What Is the economics of art and culture?. In *Economics of Art and Culture* (pp. 3–11). Cham: SpringerBriefs in Economics, Springer International Publishing. 10.1007/978-3-030-15748-7_1.

Galloway, S., & Dunlop, S. (2007). A critique of definitions of the cultural and creative industries in public policy. *International Journal of Cultural Policy,* 13(1), 17–31. 10.1080/10286630701201657.

Galuszka, P., & Brzozowska, B. (2017). Crowdfunding and the democratization of the music market. *Media, Culture & Society,* 39(6), 833–849. 10.1177/0163443716674364.

García-Quevedo, J., Jové-Llopis, E., & Martínez-Ros, E. (2020). Barriers to the circular economy in European small and medium-sized firms. *Business Strategy and the Environment,* 29(6), 2450–2464. 10.1002/bse.2513.

Geissdoerfer, M., Savaget, P., Bocken, N. M., & Hultink, E. J. (2017). The circular economy–A new sustainability paradigm?. *Journal of Cleaner Production,* 143, 757–768. 10.1016/j.jclepro.2016.12.048.

Ghisellini, P., Cialani, C., & Ulgiati, S. (2016). A review on circular economy: The expected transition to a balanced interplay of environmental and economic systems. *Journal of Cleaner Production,* 114, 11–32. 10.1016/j.jclepro.2015.09.007.

Global Entrepreneurship Monitor. (2022). *Global Entrepreneurship Monitor 2021/2022, Women's Entrepreneurship Report: From Crisis to Opportunity.* London: Global Entrepreneurship Research Association. Available at: https://gemconsortium.org/reports/womens-entrepreneurship (Retrieved on 24 November 2022).

Gundolf, K., Jaouen, A., & Gast, J. (2018). Motives for strategic alliances in cultural and creative industries. *Creativity and Innovation Management,* 27(2), 148–160. 10.1111/caim.12255.

Hervé, F., & Schwienbacher, A. (2018). Crowdfunding and innovation. *Journal of Economic Surveys,* 32(5), 1514–1530. 10.1111/joes.12274.

Hobbs, J., Grigore, G., & Molesworth, M. (2016). Success in the management of crowdfunding projects in the creative industries. *Internet Research*, 26(1), 146–166. 10.1108/IntR-08-2014-0202.

Jian, L., & Shin, J. (2015). Motivations behind donors' contributions to crowdfunded journalism. *Mass Communication and Society*, 18(2), 165–185. 10.1080/15205436.2014.911328.

Johnson, M. A., Stevenson, R. M., & Letwin, C. R. (2018). A woman's place is in the … startup! Crowdfunder judgments, implicit bias, and the stereotype content model. *Journal of Business Venturing*, 33(6), 813–831. 10.1016/j.jbusvent.2018.04.003.

Khlystova, O., Kalyuzhnova, Y., & Belitski, M. (2022). The impact of the COVID-19 pandemic on the creative industries: A literature review and future research agenda. *Journal of Business Research*, 139, 1192–1210. 10.1016/j.jbusres.2021.09.062.

Koch, J. A., & Siering, M. (2019). The recipe of successful crowdfunding campaigns. *Electronic Markets*, 29(4), 661–679. 10.1007/s12525-019-00357-8.

Laguía, A., García-Ael, C., Wach, D., & Moriano, J. A. (2019). "Think entrepreneur-think male": A task and relationship scale to measure gender stereotypes in entrepreneurship. *International Entrepreneurship and Management Journal*, 15(3), 749–772. 10.1007/s11365-018-0553-0.

Lam, P. T., & Law, A. O. (2016). Crowdfunding for renewable and sustainable energy projects: An exploratory case study approach. *Renewable and Sustainable Energy Reviews*, 60, 11–20. 10.1016/j.rser.2016.01.046.

Lieder, M., & Rashid, A. (2016). Towards circular economy implementation: A comprehensive review in context of manufacturing industry. *Journal of Cleaner Production*, 115, 36–51. 10.1016/j.jclepro.2015.12.042.

Mollick, E. (2014). The dynamics of crowdfunding: An exploratory study. *Journal of Business Venturing*, 29(1), 1–16. 10.1016/j.jbusvent.2013.06.005

Mollick, E., & Nanda, R. (2016). Wisdom or madness? Comparing crowds with expert evaluation in funding the arts. *Management Science*, 62(6), 1533–1553. 10.1287/mnsc.2015.2207.

Nucciarelli, A., Li, F., Fernandes, K. J., Goumagias, N., Cabras, I., Devlin, S., … & Cowling, P. (2017). From value chains to technological platforms: The effects of crowdfunding in the digital game industry. *Journal of Business Research*, 78, 341–352. 10.1016/j.jbusres.2016.12.030.

OECD. (2021). Economic and social impact of cultural and creative sectors. *Note for Italy G20 Presidency Culture Working Group*. Available at: https://www.oecd.org/cfe/leed/OECD-G20-Culture-July-2021.pdf (retrieved on 2 November 2022).

OECD. (2022). "Public and private funding for cultural and creative sectors", in The Culture Fix: Creative People, Places and Industries, OECD Publishing, Paris. 10.1787/29f05369-en.

Ordanini, A., Miceli, L., Pizzetti, M., & Parasuraman, A. (2011). Crowd-funding: Transforming customers into investors through innovative service platforms. *Journal of Service Management*, 22(4), 443–470. 10.1108/09564231111155079.

Pizzi, S., Corbo, L., & Caputo, A. (2021). Fintech and SMEs sustainable business models: Reflections and considerations for a circular economy. *Journal of Cleaner Production*, 281, 125217. 10.1016/j.jclepro.2020.125217.

Poczter, S., & Shapsis, M. (2018). Gender disparity in angel financing. *Small Business Economics*, 51(1), 31–55. 10.1007/s11187-017-9922-2.

Powell, G. N., Butterfield, D. A., & Parent, J. D. (2002). Gender and managerial stereotypes: Have the times changed?. *Journal of Management*, 28(2), 177–193. 10.1016/S0149-2063(01)00136-2.

Pratt, A. C., & Jeffcutt, P. (2009). Creativity, innovation and the cultural economy: Snake oil for the twenty-first century? In Andy C. Pratt and Paul Jeffcutt (eds.), *Creativity, innovation and the cultural economy* (pp. 1–20). London: Routledge.

Rubio Arostegui, J. A., & Rius-Ulldemolins, J. (2020). Cultural policies in the South of Europe after the global economic crisis: Is there a Southern model within the framework of European convergence? *International Journal of Cultural Policy*, 26(1), 16–30. 10.1080/10286632.2018.1429421.

Sigurdardottir, M. S., & Candi, M. (2019). Growth strategies in creative industries. *Creativity and Innovation Management*, 28(4), 477–485. 10.1111/caim.12334.

Testa, S., Nielsen, K. R., Bogers, M., & Cincotti, S. (2019). The role of crowdfunding in moving towards a sustainable society. *Technological Forecasting and Social Change*, 141, 66–73. 10.1016/j.techfore.2018.12.011.

Tosatto, J., Cox, J., & Nguyen, T. (2022). With a little help from my friends: The role of online creator-fan communication channels in the success of creative crowdfunding campaigns. *Computers in Human Behavior*, 127, 107005. 10.1016/j.chb.2021.107005.

Tyni, H. (2020). Double duty: Crowdfunding and the evolving game production network. *Games and Culture*, 15(2), 114–137. 10.1177/15554120177481.

Vasileiadou, E., Huijben, J. C. C. M., & Raven, R. P. J. M. (2016). Three is a crowd? Exploring the potential of crowdfunding for renewable energy in the Netherlands. *Journal of Cleaner Production*, 128, 142–155. 10.1016/j.jclepro.2015.06.028.

Wachs, J., & Vedres, B. (2021). Does crowdfunding really foster innovation? Evidence from the board game industry. *Technological Forecasting and Social Change*, 168, 120747. 10.1016/j.techfore.2021.120747.

Werthes, D., Mauer, R., & Brettel, M. (2018). Cultural and creative entrepreneurs: Understanding the role of entrepreneurial identity. *International Journal of Entrepreneurial Behavior & Research*, 24(1), 290–314. 10.1108/IJEBR-07-2016-0215.

6   Conclusions

6.1   Lessons from the past

Many new players have emerged in the entrepreneurial finance landscape in recent years, creating new opportunities for entrepreneurs and businesses to raise capital beyond the traditional forms of financing (Block *et al.*, 2018). These new players have proven their ability to provide early-stage ventures and SMEs with more flexible and customised fundraising strategies and instruments to finance their businesses (Bellavitis *et al.*, 2017). At the same time, by harnessing the power of the internet, these new players have allowed many successful innovative businesses from both developed and emerging countries to attract international investors outside of traditional Global Financial Centres, overcoming geographical barriers.

Beyond the traditional forms of financing (i.e., banks, venture capital, private equity funds, and business angels), crowdfunding can represent a driving force not only in helping micro, small, and medium-sized enterprises overcome credit constraints but also in encouraging the creation and growth of businesses in booming industries like artificial intelligence (AI), biotechnology, information technology, and communications technology. It is widely recognised by practitioners and academics that crowdfunding, together with other players in the alternative finance ecosystem, is democratising entrepreneurial finance by providing access to funding to a much larger and diversified number of businesses and entrepreneurs than was possible in the past, especially in countries where the banking system is often underdeveloped (Cumming *et al.*, 2021).

In this era of technology-driven innovation, where emerging technologies are disrupting the financial services industry, new trends, market niches, and different players have emerged and constantly continue to appear in the alternative finance landscape. FinTech companies, such as crowdfunding platforms, have become one of the main game changers in the entrepreneurial finance market; while banks and financial institutions are losing centrality in the daily lives of their customers, FinTech

DOI: 10.4324/9781003381518-7

companies are constantly scrutinising incumbents' activity in search of any potential gaps to fill. These companies are exploiting new technologies to create new organisational forms of alternative finance provision that can easily adapt to the changing needs and opportunities they uncover in the market.

In a context in which the entrepreneurial finance markets are becoming a battleground where competition is becoming increasingly intense, there are many dynamic changes to look at and be ready to deal with in the near future.

6.2 Outlook on the future of alternative finance

The future prospects of the alternative finance industry reveal its evolving nature that has created and will continue to create a wealth of new opportunities for business financing. The alternative finance landscape has grown over the past decade, showing its ability to complement traditional bank debt financing in meeting the evolving funding needs of businesses that are increasingly moving towards knowledge- and technology-based activities as a source of competitive advantage. Alternative finance has radically changed capital-raising practices, giving rise to new lending, investment, and non-investment models that allow fundraisers (i.e., individuals, businesses, and other entities) to raise funds via online platforms and funders (i.e., retail and professional investors) to finance entrepreneurial projects. Outside of the incumbent banking systems and traditional capital markets, new alternative finance ecosystems have emerged, where the once widely prevalent bank financing is coupled with independent actors that aim at providing more flexible and customised funding instruments and other financial services by making use of emerging technologies. These new actors (so-called FinTech companies), along with new digital technologies and regulations, such as the Payment Service Directive 2 (PSD2), are shaping the future of entrepreneurial finance, generating great challenges and opportunities for the banking industry.

To effectively respond to growing competition and pressure to innovate, incumbent banks have adopted different strategies. Some of them have tried to build innovative technologies themselves by increasing investments in research and development (R&D), others have established strategic alliances or ad-hoc partnerships (Hornuf *et al.*, 2021), and an increasing number of banks have decided to join forces with their FinTech competitors through mergers and acquisitions (M&As) transactions (Thakor, 2020).

In 2022, several acquisitions of FinTechs by European banks took place, including France's BNP Paribas SA's €120 million acquisition of Kantox Ltd., a British FinTech that automates foreign exchange risk management, and the acquisition by Société Générale SA of the majority stake in the British payments FinTech PayXpert Ltd. Examples of other relevant deals, that occurred in 2022, are the acquisition by Italy's Compass Banca SpA, the consumer credit arm of Mediobanca Banca di Credito Finanziario SpA, of two FinTechs in the buy-now-pay-later (BNPL) space to accelerate its growth in the segment of deferred payment on digital channels. The first was the 100% acquisition of the Italian Soisy SpA, a FinTech specialised in offering loans for online purchases, and the second was the acquisition of a 19.5% stake in the Swiss Heidi Pay Ag, a FinTech specialised in BNPL and retail financing solutions.

Belonging to the FinTech companies, crowdfunding platforms have recently started partnerships with banks. One example is represented by the strategic partnership between BNP Paribas with the donation-based crowdfunding platform Ulule in 2013 and the P2P lending platform for SMEs SmartAngles in 2016. Under the partnership with Ulule, BNP Paribas plays a dual role: it actively invests in projects launched on the platform and supports the further development of successfully funded businesses by offering them a year of free banking services and a loan of an amount equal to or greater than that collected through the platform. By partnering with SmartAngels, BNP Paribas Securities Services offers a standardisation process for financial transactions made via the platform and develops an automatic register for the financial securities issued by companies financed on SmartAngels. Working together with crowdfunding platforms has allowed BNP Paribas to grow its existing customer base more directly and on a more mass-oriented basis and provide services to more verified and trusted consumers. Another example is the partnership that took place in 2018 between the United Kingdom's leading bank Santander and the crowdfunding platform Crowdfunder to help social enterprises, small charities and community groups across the United Kingdom to access the funding they need. As part of the partnership, Santander has allocated £200,000 worth of funds which will be used to co-finance the platform's projects.

These partnerships demonstrate the complementary nature of traditional and alternative finance and pave the way for closer relationships between the banking and crowdfunding sectors.

Initial Coin Offerings or Initial Currency Offerings (hereafter, ICOs) represent an important new segment of the alternative entrepreneurial finance market that is receiving increasing attention among practitioners and academics (Block *et al.*, 2021). ICOs are a form of fundraising whereby companies (usually highly innovative blockchain ventures) or individuals sell their native digital tokens to a crowd of investors, normally in exchange for a financial contribution (Fisch, 2019). Tokens are units of value that can serve two different functions: they may grant the token holder access to a particular product or service of the issuing company or they may entitle the holder to receive dividends or other financial incentives from the company. Depending on their function, tokens may be classified as utility tokens or security tokens. Similar to reward-based crowdfunding, ICOs involving offerings of utility tokens can be started by both companies or individuals to raise capital to fund the development of their blockchain projects across a wide range of sectors. Unlike coins, utility tokens have no actual monetary value and therefore cannot be used to make investments. Investors can only use these tokens within their specific blockchain ecosystem to redeem or gain access to the company's specific product or service. Security tokens are fungible tokens (i.e., they hold monetary value) and can be seen as a digital representation of real-world assets, like bonds, stocks, or, in some cases, even gold. ICOs involving offerings of security tokens are called Security Token Offerings (STOs), and similar to equity-based crowdfunding, are limited to firms as they involve the issuance of debt or equity securities. For this reason, STOs are larger in terms of the funding amounts raised than ICOs and are subject to federal securities regulations (Kher *et al.*, 2020). ICOs are shaping the entrepreneurial finance landscape, enabling the financing of previously excluded projects, creating opportunities for new organisational forms of alternative finance provision that challenge existing models of corporate governance, and contributing to the building of a digital sharing economy for sustainable development.

6.3 Questions still to be answered

As alternative finance markets grow around the world and undergo profound transformations, several questions arise whose answers are not directly derivable (easily transferrable) from other types of entrepreneurial finance.

The future of alternative finance and the tangible disruption of traditional banks and financial institutions: where is the ceiling and will we break through it?

In a world characterised by the most disruptive evolution in new digital technologies since the advent of the internet decades ago, entrepreneurial finance has seen a structural shift away from traditional forms of funding to other non-traditional alternatives. The use of advanced technologies, such as AI, machine learning, blockchain, robotics, and the Internet of Things (IoT), has changed the status quo, reshaping the European financial services industry (Financial Stability Board, 2017). As alternative finance emerged from the shadows, new players have entered the entrepreneurial finance landscape, offering faster, more accessible, and better-personalised products and services, automated lending processes, simplified ways to assess credit risk and determine loan terms, and more (Block *et al.*, 2018). In this evolving context, banks and traditional financial institutions must understand the urgency of modernising their core business activities and services based on off-the-shelf solutions and outdated legacy technologies and rethink their role and function in the market (Basel Committee on Banking Supervision, 2018).

From a managerial perspective will the evolution of the alternative finance market in Europe support businesses, especially SMEs and startups, in the transition towards a circular economy?

Although the shift towards more sustainable production and consumption models has become increasingly and urgently important to the global agenda (del Mar Alonso-Almeida *et al.*, 2021), the lack of external capital still remains a major deterrent for businesses (Ormazabal *et al.*, 2018; Sharma *et al.*, 2021). With the exception of large companies and start-ups born under the circular economy paradigm, fuelling circular business models (i.e., models aimed at creating value for stakeholders while reducing ecological and social costs to a minimum) is not easy and requires a considerable amount of financial resources (Goovaerts *et al.*, 2018; Pizzi *et al.*, 2021). Traditional banks and financial institutions play a central role in accelerating the transition to a circular economy by providing the appropriate financial resources, adequate financial schemes, and professional financial advisory services. However, often early-stage ventures and SMEs do not present the profiles to attract debt financing as they do not have the required collateral or are unable to show bankers their potential.

In addition, these companies often fail to attract even equity investors, such as venture capitalists and business angels, as they are unlikely to scale up in short periods of time (Gaddy *et al.*, 2017). Additionally, European, national, and local grants that support circular initiatives often prove inadequate to provide the right amounts of funding to boost a change towards more life-cycle-oriented entrepreneurship (Demirel and Danisman, 2019).

In this context, alternative financing sources, such as crowdfunding, could better suit the needs of early-stage ventures and SMEs, financially constrained in traditional financial markets, to access capital to achieve a successful transition to the circular economy.

What are the next challenges for alternative finance?

Like any other industry, alternative finance faces a number of challenges to secure its longevity, which entrepreneurs and investors need to be aware of.

• Regulation
  Regulation is still a primary hurdle in alternative finance. While national and supranational laws continue to evolve, the regulatory landscape is still complex. This makes it difficult for entrepreneurs and investors to understand the various alternative finance models available and how they work.

- Lack of liquidity
  The lack of well-functioning secondary trading markets, whose main objective is to create liquidity for investors by allowing them to sell their shares and recover their money, decreases investor participation in alternative finance and therefore the amount of capital available for businesses (Lukkarinen and Schwienbacher, 2023). Providing viable exit opportunities for investors remains an important missing part of alternative finance.
- Difficulty in assessing risks
  Investments in alternative finance can involve a higher degree of risk than traditional investments (Yasar, 2021). They can be highly speculative and volatile, resulting in significant gains or losses for investors. They may have more complex valuation and return metrics. They may lack transparency and provide limited reliable information which makes due diligence and decision-making more challenging. Alternative investments may be subject to less regulation and charge higher fees.
- Preserve its nature and values
  Alternative finance is designed to be flexible, not constrained by legacy systems or burdensome regulation. As the industry matures and digital platforms get bigger, the challenge is to avoid distorting the authentic meaning of alternative finance and the sense of revolution that it brings with it.

References

Basel Committee on Banking Supervision. (2018). Sound practices: Implications of fintech developments for banks and bank supervisors. Available at: https://www.bis.org/bcbs/publ/d431.pdf (retrieved on 27 October 2023).

Bellavitis, C., Filatotchev, I., Kamuriwo, D. S., & Vanacker, T. (2017). Entrepreneurial finance: New frontiers of research and practice: Editorial for the special issue Embracing entrepreneurial funding innovations. *Venture Capital*, 19(1-2), 1–16. 10.1080/13691066.2016.1259733.

Block, J. H., Colombo, M. G., Cumming, D. J., & Vismara, S. (2018). New players in entrepreneurial finance and why they are there. *Small Business Economics*, 50, 239–250. 10.1007/s11187-016-9826-6.

Block, J. H., Groh, A., Hornuf, L., Vanacker, T., & Vismara, S. (2021). The entrepreneurial finance markets of the future: A comparison of crowdfunding and initial coin offerings. *Small Business Economics*, 57(2), 865–882. 10.1007/s11187-020-00330-2.

Cumming, D., Meoli, M., & Vismara, S. (2021). Does equity crowdfunding democratize entrepreneurial finance? *Small Business Economics*, 56, 533–552. 10.1007/s11187-019-00188-z.

del Mar Alonso-Almeida, M., Rodriguez-Anton, J. M., Bagur-Femenías, L., & Perramon, J. (2021). Institutional entrepreneurship enablers to promote circular economy in the European Union: Impacts on transition towards a more circular economy. *Journal of Cleaner Production*, 281, 124841. 10.1016/j.jclepro.2020.124841.

Demirel, P., & Danisman, G. O. (2019). Eco-innovation and firm growth in the circular economy: Evidence from European small-and medium-sized enterprises. *Business Strategy and the Environment*, 28(8), 1608–1618. 10.1002/bse.2336.

Financial Stability Board. (2017). Financial stability implications from FinTech. Supervisory and regulatory issues that merit authorities' attention. Available at: https://www.fsb.org/wp-content/uploads/R270617.pdf (retrieved on 27 October 2023).

Fisch, C. (2019). Initial coin offerings (ICOs) to finance new ventures. *Journal of Business Venturing*, 34(1), 1–22. 10.1016/j.jbusvent.2018.09.007

Gaddy, B. E., Sivaram, V., Jones, T. B., & Wayman, L. (2017). Venture capital and cleantech: The wrong model for energy innovation. *Energy Policy*, 102, 385–395. 10.1016/j.enpol.2016.12.035.

Goovaerts, L., Schempp, C., Busato, L., Smits, A., Žutelija, L., & Piechocki, R. (2018). Financing innovation and circular economy. In E. Benetto, K. Gericke, & M. Guiton (eds.), *Designing Sustainable Technologies, Products and Policies: From Science to Innovation* (pp. 427–432). Cham: Springer. 10.1007/978-3-319-66981-6_47.

Hornuf, L., Klus, M. F., Lohwasser, T. S., & Schwienbacher, A. (2021). How do banks interact with fintech startups?. *Small Business Economics*, 57(3), 1505–1526. 10.1007/s11187-020-00359-3.

Kher, R., Terjesen, S., & Liu, C. (2020). Blockchain, Bitcoin, and ICOs: A review and research agenda. *Small Business Economics*, 56, 1699–1720. 10.1007/s111 87-019-00286-y.

Lukkarinen, A., & Schwienbacher, A. (2023). Secondary market listings in equity crowdfunding: The missing link? *Research Policy*, 52(1), 104648. 10.1016/j.respol.2022.104648.

Ormazabal, M., Prieto-Sandoval, V., Puga-Leal, R., & Jaca, C. (2018). Circular economy in Spanish SMEs: Challenges and opportunities. *Journal of Cleaner Production*, 185, 157–167. 10.1016/j.jclepro.2018.03.031.

Pizzi, S., Corbo, L., & Caputo, A. (2021). Fintech and SMEs sustainable business models: Reflections and considerations for a circular economy. *Journal of Cleaner Production*, 281, 125217. 10.1016/j.jclepro.2020.125217.

Sharma, N. K., Govindan, K., Lai, K. K., Chen, W. K., & Kumar, V. (2021). The transition from linear economy to circular economy for sustainability among SMEs: A study on prospects, impediments, and prerequisites. *Business Strategy and the Environment*, 30(4), 1803–1822. 10.1002/bse.2717.

Thakor, A. V. (2020). Fintech and banking: What do we know? *Journal of Financial Intermediation*, 41, 100833. 10.1016/j.jfi.2019.100833.

Yasar, B. (2021). The new investment landscape: Equity crowdfunding. *Central Bank Review*, 21(1), 1–16. 10.1016/j.cbrev.2021.01.001.

Index

Note: page numbers in **bold** refer to tables

118 *Index*

Printed in the United States
by Baker & Taylor Publisher Services